INSIGHT *Pocket*

ST. PETERSBURG

Белые ночи
White Nights

APA PUBLICATIONS

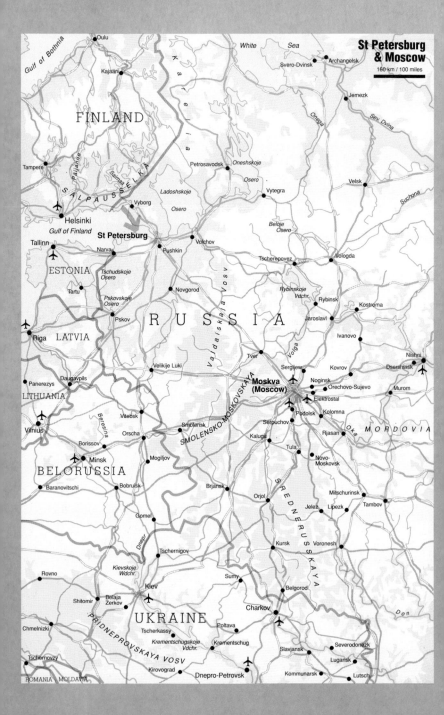

Dear Visitor!

Since its days as Peter the Great's 'window on the West' St Petersburg has been the most compelling Russian city for travellers. With its fabulous tsarist palaces and wealth of literary and musical associations, it rewards detailed exploration.

In these pages *Insight Guides'* correspondent in St Petersburg, Anna Benn, has devised a range of itineraries to bring you the best of the city. Three full-day tours combine all the essential sights, while eight Pick & Mix options and three excursions into the Russian countryside cater to visitors with more time. Chapters on shopping, eating out and nightlife are followed by a fact-packed practical information section.

 Anna Benn first went to St Petersburg (then called Leningrad) as a student, when the movements of foreigners were strictly controlled: 'We were all given strict warnings – don't do this, it is forbidden to do that,' Anna recalls. 'In fact there was little we could do except work, and the Russians certainly worked us.' Despite some initial paranoia – she thought the radio in her bedroom was bugged – her first few months in St Petersburg proved fascinating and led to a deep affection for the city and all things Russian. Anna's advice to first-time visitors today is to take a sense of humour with them, because, she says, 'an element of madness keeps the place afloat.'

Hans Höfer.
Publisher, Insight Guides

C O N T E N T S

Pages 2/3:
St Petersburg from
St Isaac's Cathedral

Pages 8/9:
Young cadets

HISTORY

'*To* understand our country you have to understand her past' – Mikhail Gorbachev

When you arrive in this city, you may well approach it from the outskirts, passing tall, monotonous grey buildings of the Soviet era and crowds of people squeezing themselves onto buses or queuing for provisions outside dreary-looking shops.

Then suddenly you pass through an invisible barrier and the streets change their character, the buildings are older, the colour scheme changes from grey to pastel shades – pale greens, yellows, pinks, terracottas and gold – and all at once you feel as if you have gone back into the 19th century. There are statues, beautiful railings, canals, and landscapes of perfectly proportioned buildings. At this moment you realise that the outskirts you have left were Leningrad and you have entered St Petersburg.

St Petersburg in the 19th century

Peter the Great

Peter the Great and Lenin were responsible for the city's two names – even though 'Sankt Pietr' was actually a Dutch saint. And though Lenin moved the capital to Moscow, his presence remained in the streets long after he had gone – huge statues, museums, flags, slogans proclaiming 'all power to the Soviets'.

But where is he now? He's disappeared overnight. You decide you want to go to a Lenin museum, find out a bit more about the Revolution, but it's gone... No, you are told, this building used to house the museum of the October Revolution but before that it was a palace; a well-known prince, Grand Duke, writer or ballerina lived here first. It's now their museum or it's an art gallery.

The traces of Lenin may be disappearing, but the giant founder of the city, Peter the Great, is ever present, sitting on his bronze horse beside the River Neva. The speed with which he created the city has been matched only by the speed of events since his time. Millions upon millions have died here and the city rests on the bones of its builders. St Petersburg has seen uprisings and palace coups, revolutions, murders, hunger and wars – one of which reduced it to a shell. But no sooner has it been destroyed, than it patiently rebuilds itself, step by step.

The Tsars

Peter the Great, Russia's best-known ruler, had a passion for Europe and for the sea. Before he founded St Petersburg he had travelled incognito to Europe and worked in her shipyards. Russia had been and would continue to be at war with Sweden for years, but in 1709 he managed to secure a Swedish defeat at Poltava. The Peter and Paul Fortress had been built in 1703, but it was only after Poltava that the development of the city began. A vital port which controlled the Baltic Sea now lay in Russian hands, and what began as a military base soon turned into a cosmopolitan capital – St Petersburg.

Architects were invited from all over Europe and a massive Russian workforce settled in to execute his strict and organised plans, which did not allow for any architectural idiosyncracies. All roads were to be straight. The city was to be Russia's window onto Europe. Although the land on which it was built had been sparsely populated it was not an obvious base on which to build a major city, consisting of lowland, thick forest and swamp as well as having a harsh climate. Peter was not deterred, and the city of wood and stone rose up almost overnight. The intended centre was Vasilievsky Island but in time the town centre moved, almost jumped, to the opposite bank.

Catherine the Great

After Peter's death the city was somewhat neglected, but his daughter, the Empress Elizabeth, and his 'spiritual' daughter, Catherine the Great, saw to its completion, although they did not follow his style. Both chose their own architects, Western like his, and left their own distinctive imprints. Elizabeth decorated extravagantly, almost coquettishly, with baroque and rococo, adding colour, chintz, mirrors and gold (the Catherine Palace at Tsarskoe Selo is a good example of her taste). Catherine influenced the city in a major way. Many historians maintain that she was responsible for completing the major imperial city that Peter had envisaged. She bridged the river and covered the embankments with granite, leaving a more serious, imposing trace of classicism; this reached its peak during the reign of Alexander I, when buildings such as the General Staff headquarters in Palace Square and the Napoleonic column to mark Russia's defeat of Bonaparte were erected.

The official religion of the time was Russian Orthodoxy, which enjoyed special privileges and rights. The churches were built by the same architects who designed the palaces.

Art and Commerce

Art flourished in the 19th century, and the city produced some of the greatest writers in world literature, such as Dostoevsky, Gogol

and Pushkin. The St Petersburg Conservatory was established in 1862, and its musicians include Tchaikovsky, Borodin, Mussorgsky and Rimsky-Korsakov. The Russian ballet was born here under Empress Anna and the Imperial Ballet School founded, where famous dancers such as Pavlova and Nijinsky were trained. Few countries in the world pay such homage to their writers and artists – an irony in a place which has also so severely repressed them. This is reflected in the way that their flats and houses have been turned into literary museums, faithfully restored as shrines to the past.

From the beginning of the 19th century St Petersburg grew into a rich industrial centre attracting foreign firms such as Siemens-Schuckert, Thornton, Fabergé and the Singer Sewing Machine company, as well as establishing its own. The railways were built in the time of Nicholas I, the first of which was the line to Tsarskoe Selo from what is now the Vitebsk Station. Russia's might was not just reflected in the architecture of the city, but in the opulent lifestyle of the Tsars, which alienated them from the people, peasants, workers and intellectuals alike. Not surprisingly, revolutionary organisations sprang up, starting with the first Decembrist uprising of 1825, followed by the emergence of populism amongst the intelligensia, and the terrorism of the People's Will Party which finally assassinated Tsar Alexander II after several failed attempts. He had tried to liberalise the system by freeing the serfs, moderating the legal system and creating new rural councils – but the people demanded more. Any insurrection was ruthlessly put down and the offenders jailed in the Peter and Paul Fortress, which became the symbol of Tsarist oppression.

Both Alexander III

Dostoevsky: St Petersburg writer

Nicholas II, the last Tsar

and Nicholas II tried to hold the autocratic regime together as insurrection mounted. Industrialisation brought about bad living conditions, the cause of massive discontent amongst an expanding workforce. Russia suffered a disastrous defeat in Japan. The general ill-feeling erupted in a series of revolts which Lenin later regarded as a 'dress rehearsal' for the October 1917 Revolution. An uprising led by a priest, Father Gapon, whose message was one of despair, was crushed outside the Winter Palace and the event became known as 'Bloody Sunday'. The dead lie buried in the Field of Mars.

After the first revolution of 1905 concessions were made by the state and a parliament or *Duma* was set up, the running of which was interrupted by World War I. In the wave of anti-German sentiment the war provoked, the German-sounding St Petersburg was renamed Petrograd.

It wasn't until 1917, after massive strikes and demonstrations, that Nicholas II was forced to abdicate and the Romanov dynasty came to an end.

The Cradle of the Revolution

Lenin arrived at the Finland Station in 1917 where he addressed

the people from the top of an armoured car. On the night of 17 October the Bolshevik Party seized power, entering the Winter Palace and capturing the Provisional Government. The battleship *Aurora* fired the empty shell that heralded the Revolution. Promising peace, land to the peasants and power to the workers, Lenin formed the world's first communist state.

Three years of civil war followed the Revolution. In 1918 Lenin moved the capital to Moscow. When

Revolutionary reading

he died in 1924, Petrograd was renamed Leningrad. Socialist urban reconstruction, when factories and new residential areas were built, marked the years until the onset of World War II.

Stalin's Russia witnessed repression, purges and terror. The city grew and local industry reached its pre-war level of production. Fearing Leningrad as a powerful political rival, Stalin had the local communist leader, Sergei Kirov, assassinated (the ballet was renamed after his death in 1935), and the purges began. Then came the German invasion and the 900-day siege of the city. Leningrad lost thousands of its people through air raids and shelling, but many more through starvation.

In memory of war

The outstanding poets living and working in St Petersburg before and after the Revolution were Alexander Blok, whose famous poem 'The Twelve' powerfully brings to life the days of Revolution, and Anna Akhmatova, who wrote at the height of Stalinist terror. The houses in which they lived are now open to the public. The musician Dmitry Shostakovich composed his Seventh Symphony during the wartime blockade and it was first performed in the Philharmonic Hall in the city's Square of the Arts.

Tourism and the Present Day

Modern visitors did not appear in the city until the late 1950s when the Stalinist system was discredited under Khruschev, several years after Stalin's death.

Intourist has dominated the travel scene for years, although other travel organisations have emerged. Under St Petersburg's mayor, Anatoly Sobchak, money is being spent on tourism. The population is now roughly 5 million.

To the foreigner, it appears that the city is, as in the time of Peter the Great, looking to the culture of the West. Western firms and joint ventures are cropping up everywhere and the word 'businessman' has entered the Russian vocabulary untranslated. It is becoming harder to distinguish a Westerner from a foreigner in the street. The crime rate, the mafia and prostitution have increased dramatically and people complain of the lowering of standards, of litter, decay and pollution. What has happened to literature, people ask... how can our young be educated when all they can buy are crime and sex books? But despite its borrowings from the West, St Petersburg has its own lively art and music scene which had its beginnings in the underground culture of the communist era.

With the exception of a few – those who have access to Western currency (and Russian millionaires are not unheard of now) – the people complain of worse living conditions than ever before. Families are selling their clothes to *kommissioniy* shops and stand in the streets selling off their bric-à-brac. If you stop to listen to conversations in the street, nine times out of ten they will be about money, of the ridiculous levels of inflation and cost of food. People are not interested in the reforms brought about by *glasnost* so long as they are unable to live off their meagre wages and pensions. Food comes before freedom of speech.

Housing conditions are cramped in St Petersburg, where it is the norm to share a flat with several other families. It is a different story outside the town, where many people have *dachas*, small wooden huts, and the transition between life in the city and the country is startling. The Russians make great use of natural resources and in June and July there is a frenzy of jam making and an abundance of different berries. In September everyone rushes out to the fields to pick mushrooms.

Despite the hardships, life goes on. It is still an inspiring and fascinating city to visit. One of the most pleasurable things about tourism today is that you can wander freely around the city and speak openly on subjects which were strictly taboo in the past. You can now stay with Russian friends, although the complicated visa system whereby you have to receive an invitation if you wish to travel independently restricts spontaneous travel. How far down the path of Westernisation this city will go before the end of the 20th century remains to be seen. Anything can happen here – as history has shown.

The face of St Petersburg today

Historical Highlights

9th century Creation of first Russian state, centred on city of Kiev. The borders of the northern lands, 'Upper Rus', where St Petersburg was later to be founded, were fought over for seven centuries by Russians and Swedes.

1240 First famous battle on the Neva. Alexander of Novgorod defeats Swedes and becomes Alexander Nevsky.

1682 Birth of Peter (I) the Great.

1700–21 Great Northern War with Sweden.

16 May 1703 Peter and Paul Fortress completed.

1709 Peter defeats the Swedes at the Battle of Poltava. Development of the city begins in earnest. Over 100,000 soldiers and peasants are recruited to start work. City is named "Sankt Pieter Burkh" – Saint Peter's city. The building of Petrodvoretz, the Twelve Colleges and the Menshikov Palace is now well under way.

1712 The court moves north from Moscow to the new capital. Russia becomes a major European power.

1725–62 Peter the Great's death is followed by reigns of Catherine I and Peter II. Both preferred Moscow. Anna Ivanovna takes up residence in St Petersburg which, during her reign and that of her successor, Elizabeth, grows rapidly. Winter Palace, Smolny Cathedral and Catherine Palace completed under the architect Rastrelli.

1762–96 Catherine the Great. Hermitage and Academy of Arts founded.

1796–1801 Paul I. Pavlovsk built.

1801–25 Alexander I's reign dominated by the Napoleonic War. Building of Smolny Institute, the Mikhail Palace, the General Staff buildings.

1825–55 Nicholas I.

December 1825 Decembrist uprising crushed. Railway between Moscow and St Petersburg built. Russian defeat in Crimean War. Completion of St Isaac's Cathedral.

1855–81 Alexander II. Great reforms and abolition of serfdom. Emergence of People's Will Party, responsible for assassination of Tsar on banks of Griboedova canal.

1881–94 Alexander III.

1894–1917 Nicholas II. Emergence of growing opposition from populist, Marxist and liberal groups. St Petersburg develops into large industrial city.

1914–24 Renamed Petrograd because of anti-German sentiment. Mass demonstrations, mutinies. Provisional and Soviet Government formed. Abdication of Tsar.

1917 Lenin seizes power in October. Revolution followed by three years of civil war.

1918 Capital moves to Moscow.

1924 Lenin's death, Petrograd renamed Leningrad.

1941 German invasion and start of Great Patriotic War. In September the 900-day siege of the city begins. Death toll of over 650,000.

1943 Blockade broken.

1945 Reconstruction begins.

1953 Death of Stalin. Cultural thaw and the principle of 'peaceful coexistence'.

1957–64 Nikita Khruschev. Policy of de-Stalinization.

1964–82 Leonid Brezhnev.

1982–5 Yuri Andropov, Konstantin Chernenko.

1985–91 Mikhail Gorbachev becomes president.

1991 Resistance to attempted coup against Gorbachev in Moscow (August) headed by the mayor, Anatoly Sobchak, in St Petersburg. 100,000 demonstrate in Palace Square. In September Leningrad renamed St Petersburg. Resignation of Mikhail Gorbachev in December.

1992 Boris Yeltsin president.

December 1993 First free Russian parliamentary elections since 1917.

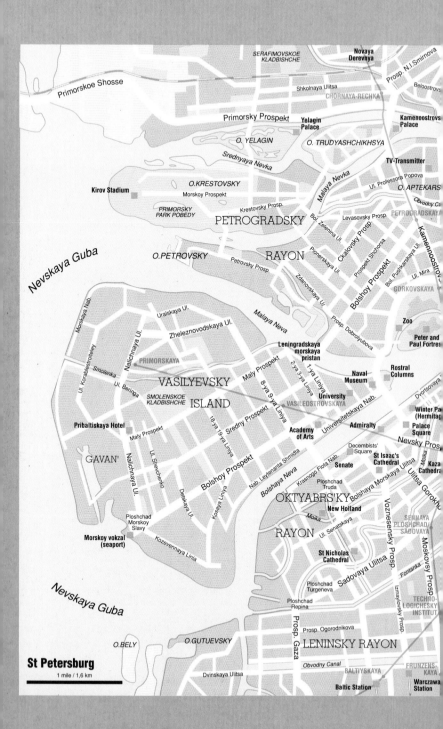

St Petersburg

1 mile / 1,6 km

SERAFIMOVSKOE KLADBISHCHE

Novaya Derevnya

Prosp. N.I.Smirnova

Beloostrov

Primorskoe Shosse

Shkolnaya Ulitsa

CHORNAYA RECHKA

Primorsky Prospekt

Yelagin Palace

Kamenoostrovsky Palace

O. YELAGIN

O. TRUDYASHCHIKHSYA

TV-Transmitter

Srednyaya Nevka

Malaya Nevka

Ul. Professora Popova

O. APTEKARS

Kirov Stadium

O.KRESTOVSKY

Morskoy Prospekt

Obvodny Ca

Krestovsky Prosp.

PRIMORSKY PARK POBEDY

Levasovsky Prosp.

PETROGRADSKY

PETROGRADSKY

Bol. Zelenina Ul.

Ckalovsky Prosp.

Prospekt Shchorsa

Nevskaya Guba

O.PETROVSKY

RAYON

Petrovsky Prosp.

Pionerskaya Ul.

Bolshoy Prospekt

Bol. Pushkarskaya Ul.

Ul. Mira

GORKOVSKAYA

Zdanovskaya Ul.

Prosp. Dobrolyubova

Uralskaya Ul.

Zheleznovodskaya Ul.

Malaya Neva

Zoo

Peter and Paul Fortres

Morskaya Nab.

Nalichnaya Ul.

PRIMORSKAYA

Leningradskaya morskaya pristan

Rostral Columns

Dvortsov

Smolenka

Ul. Korablestroiteley

Ul. Beringa

VASILYEVSKY

Maly Prospekt

2-ya 3-ya Liniya

1-ya Liniya

Naval Museum

Winter Pa (Hermitag

SMOLENSKOE KLADBISHCHE

ISLAND

VASILEOSTROVSKAYA

University

Palace Square

Pribaltiskaya Hotel

Maly Prospekt

18-ya 19-ya Liniya

Sredny Prospekt

8-ya 9-ya Liniya

Universitetskaya Nab.

Academy of Arts

Admiralty

Nevsky Pros.

GAVAN'

Nalichnaya Ul.

Ul. Shevchenko

Bolshoy Prospekt

Kosaya Liniya

Nab. Leytenanta Shmidta

Bolshaya Neva

Krasnogo Flota Nab.

Decembists' Square

Senate

St Isaac's Cathedral

Bolshaya Morskaya Ulitsa

Kaza Cathedra

Ul. Gorokho

Moika

Ploshchad Truda

OKTYABRSKY

New Holland

Voznesensky Prosp.

SENNAYA PLOSHCHAD/ SADOVAYA

Ploshchad Morskoy Slavy

Destskaya Ul.

Kozevennaya Linia

RAYON

Ul. Senatskaya

Moika

Moskovsky Prosp.

Morskoy vokzal (seaport)

St Nicholas Cathedral

Sadovaya Ulitsa

Izmaylovsky Prosp.

Fontanka

Nevskaya Guba

Ploshchad Turgeneva

Ploshchad Repina

Prosp. Ogorodnikova

TECHNO-LOGICHESKY INSTITUT

O.BELY

O.GUTUEVSKY

LENINSKY RAYON

Prosp. Gaza

Obvodny Canal

BALTIYSKAYA

FRUNZENS-KAYA

Dvinskaya Ulitsa

Baltic Station

Warczawa Station

Kushelevka

Polyustrovsky Prospekt

KUSHELEVKA

BOGOSLOVSKOE
KLADBISHCHE

Piskarevka

Prosp. Mechnikova

Pisarovskoye
Memorial
Cemetery

Volgo-Donskoy Prosp.

Ovskaya Ul.

LESNAYA

Prospekt Marshala Blyukhera

Samsonievsky

**KALININSKY
RAYON**

Chugunnaya Ul.

Prospekt Metallistov

Polyustrovsky Prospekt

Ul. Zukova

POLYUSTROVO

KRASNOGVARDEYSKY

RAYON

Ul. Tukhachevskovo

Prosp. Energetikov

PARK IM.
50-LETIYA
OKTYABRYA

VYBORGSKAYA

Prospekt

Lesnoy Prospekt

PLOSHCHAD
LENINA

**Finland
Station**

Ulitsa Komsomola

Neva

Sverdlovskaya Nab.

Shosse Revolyucii

Sredneokhtinsky Prosp.

Prospekt Metallistov

Industrialny Prosp.

Irinovsky Prosp.

Cruiser
Aurora
Wooden cabin

Arsenalnaya Nab.

Liteyny bridge

**Smolny
Cathedral**

Nab. Robespiera

Ploshchad
Rastrelli

BOL'SHEOKHTINSKOE
KLADBISHCHE

Bolshogorskaya Ulitsa

Nab. Kutuzova

Shpalernaya Ulitsa

Smolny Institute

Summer
Palace

CHERNYSHEVSKAYA

**Taurida
Palace**

GORODSKOY
DETSKY PARK

Yakornaya Ul.

Prosp. Energetikov

Bolshaya Okhta

Marble
Palace

Sadovaya Ul.

Panteleymons-
kaya Ulitsa

Ul. Saltykova-Shchedrina

DZERZHINSKY

Ul. Nekrasova

Suvorovsky Prosp.

Bolsheokhtinsky bridge

Krasnogvardeysky Pr.

MALOKHTA

Liteyny Prospekt

Ul. Moiseenko

Nizhegorodskaya Ul.

Sinopskaya Nab.

Malookhtinsky Prospekt

Church of
Resurrection
Ploshchad
Iskusstvo

RAYON

PLOSHCHAD
VOSSTANIYA

SMOL'NINSKY

Dacha
Dolgorukova

LADOZHSKOE

SKY PROSPEKT
TINNYDVOR

MAYAKOVSKAYA

Ploshchad
Znamenskaya

Prosp. Bakunina

RAYON

Zanevsky Prospekt

Krasnogvardeysky Prosp.

KRASNOG-
VARDEYSKAYA

Grantnaya Ul.

UYBYSHEVSKY

Ul. Lomonosova

**Moscow
Station**

Nevsky Prospekt

PLOSHCHAD
ALEXANDRA
NEVSKOVO

AYON

Zagorodny Prospekt

Mirgorodskaya Ul

Mansion
f Lenin

Ul. Marata

VLADIMIRSKAYA/
DOSTDEVSKAYA

PUSHKINSKAYA

**Alexander
Nevsky
Monastery**

Ul. Kollonntay

Vitebsk
Station

Ligovsky Prospekt

Dnepropetrovskaya Ulitsa

Obvodny Canal

Glinyanaya Ul.

Prospekt Obukhovsky

Oktyabrskaya Nab.

Dalnevostochny Prosp.

Iskrovsky Prosp.

Rybinskaya Ul.

Borovaya Ulitsa

Tambovskaya Ulitsa

Ul. Professora Kachalova

Krnostalnaya Ul.

Neva

Navalochnaya

VOLKOVO
KLADBISHCHE

If you had only three days in St Petersburg, where would you go? The three day itineraries proposed here try to answer this question by combining the most obvious sights with the slightly more off-beat. These tours are best done on foot, although, depending on where you are staying, you will need to get to your starting point by some means of transport. It is worth mastering the metro system although I would recommend a taxi until you get to know the town better.

Don't be daunted when you hear that the city stands on 101 islands. In reality, you will only be aware of the main three – the first can be called 'the mainland', the second Vasilievsky and the third Petrograd. Once you have taken a trip to the top of St Isaac's Cathedral you will have a pretty good idea of the layout.

The main street, the Nevsky Prospekt, begins at the Admiralty, the former administrative area which comprises the Winter Palace (Hermitage) and Palace Square. The Nevsky is intersected by three major waterways serviced by boat transport. On your first two days you will nearly always be in sight of the Admiralty spire.

As the palaces are such a spectacular and integral part of a visit to St Petersburg, on day three the trip takes you half an hour out of the city to one of the finest.

Make sure you check the opening times of museums and restaurants. Each museum has one day in the week when it is shut and, to complicate matters further, there is a day at the end of each month when it closes again. I have given the most up-to-date information available, but St Petersburg is changing day by day, and no book can hope to fully keep pace with these changes.

Boat transport

DIARIES

DAY 1

The Major Landmarks

A visit to the Bronze Horseman, the Admiralty, St Isaac's Cathedral, the Moika River, the Literary Café, and the State Hermitage Museum; it is advisable to book a table for lunch in the Literary Café (tel: 312 6057/7137) . This itinerary leads through the once most fashionable part of the city, and the major administrative centre. The most spectacular architecture is found here.

—Take a taxi to Ploshchad Dekabristov/Senatskaya Ploshchad (Decembrists' Square).—

The taxi will drop you in the square where the most important statue in the city stands, that of Peter the Great on a rearing horse.

It would be impossible to underestimate the historical and literary importance of this statue. It represents a symbol of the conflicting ideas about the town's founder. For example, Pushkin felt it was threatening. In his famous poem,'The Bronze Horseman', the figure comes to life and bears down on a poor clerk, Evgeny. The cost of lives in building this city, and the speed with which Peter pushed for its completion, has certainly never been forgotten and for some, the menacing nature of this statue serves as a reminder. It was cast from a model by the French sculptor, E M Falconet, and completed in 1782. Although it is

Peter the Great

The Menshikov Palace

always described as Falconet's masterpiece, it is worth pointing out that the head of the Tsar was actually modelled by one of Falconet's pupils, Marie Collot.

The square in which you are now standing – **Decembrists' Square** – was where, in 1825, Nicholas I's bodyguard fired on some 3,000 soldiers (and spectators) many of whom were innocently forced into action by revolutionary-minded young officers to protest against Nicholas I's nomination as Tsar.

To your left as you face the river are the yellow buildings of the Senate and the Synod, built by the Italian architect Carlo Rossi in 1829-32. Most of Rossi's buildings are painted yellow, as are many of the government institutions in the city. 'Yellow House' soon came to mean 'mad house' and for many Russians, a yellow building means little other than this.

Directly in front of you, across the river, is the embankment of Vasilievsky Island, the University Embankment on which stands the yellow Menshikov palace, the red University building, and, further to the right, the green and white Kunstkamera (Anthropological Museum) which you can visit on another day.

When you have looked at the Bronze Horseman for long enough, with the Neva behind you, walk towards the enormous gold dome of St Isaac's Cathedral. Bear left through the Gorky/Alexander Gardens. The first statue you come to is of the Asiatic explorer,

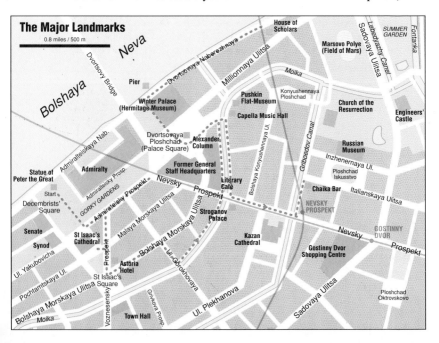

The Major Landmarks

0.8 miles / 500 m

St Isaac's Cathedral

Przhevalski (who bears an astonishing resemblance to Stalin). Keep going until you come to the fountain in front of the **Admiralty** with its statues of the writers Nikolai Gogol and Mikhail Lermontov, the composer Mikhail Glinka and the poet Vasily Zhukovsky. This was one of the first buildings in the city, constructed in 1705, and then replaced in 1806-23 by the neo-classical structure you see today from the designs of the architect A D Sakharov. It was used as a naval headquarters and a shipyard. At the top of the spire is a weather-vane in the form of a ship – the emblem of St Petersburg. From the Admiralty the main streets – Nevsky, Gorokhovaya and Vosnesensky Prospekt stretch out like an open fan.

Now, with the Admiralty behind you, and the yellow building with marble lions to your right, walk up Vosnesensky Prospekt directly in front of you into St Isaac's Square with the cathedral on your right. To buy your ticket you will need to locate the KACCA or ticket office (open 11am–6pm, closed Wednesday.) It should be signed outside the cathedral. Remember to ask for an extra ticket for the *colonnady*. This takes you up a long winding spiral staircase (562 steps) to the dome, from where you have an incredible panoramic view of the city. If you don't like heights, there is plenty to see in the cathedral itself.

St Isaac's Cathedral was built by the French architect, Auguste de Montferrand, during the reign of Alexander I. It took some 40 years to build at a great cost in lives and considerable expense. The dome is covered with 100kg (220lb) of pure gold and 43 types of stone and marble were used to decorate the interiors – you will not fail to notice the lapis lazuli and malachite columns of the iconostasis as well as the many murals. Look out for the statue of Montferrand himself, holding a model of his cathedral, a fitting tribute to the architect to whom Alexander II refused the right of burial in one of the crypts.

In the middle of the square is a statue of Nicholas I on a prancing

St Isaac's dome

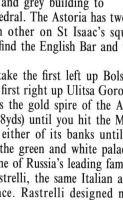

horse, by Baron Klodt. The Russians have a saying which links this statue with the Bronze Horseman, 'The fool [Nicholas I] runs after the wise man [Peter I], but St Isaac's stands in between'.

Now it's time for a quick break. Relax in comfort in one of the bars of the **Astoria Hotel**, the terracotta and grey building to your left as you come out of the cathedral. The Astoria has two entrances, within a few yards of each other on St Isaac's square. Through the first entrance, you will find the English Bar and there is another bar through the second.

Turn left out of the Astoria and take the first left up Bolshaya Morskaya Ulitsa (Gertzena). Take the first right up Ulitsa Gorokhovaya (Dzherzhinskaya). Behind you is the gold spire of the Admiralty. Keep walking (about 300m/328yds) until you hit the Moika River. Turn left and proceed along either of its banks until you come to the main thoroughfare and the green and white palace to your right, which was the home of one of Russia's leading families, the Stroganovs, and the work of Rastrelli, the same Italian architect who designed the Winter Palace. Rastrelli designed many buildings in this city, and they always stand out, with their fanciful, baroque style.

You have now reached the Nevsky Prospekt. Directly opposite you at No 18 is the yellow building of the Café Literaturnoye, the **Literary Café**, an elegant and comfortable place to have lunch. You can either pay in roubles or in hard currency and they may require an entrance fee as you go in. If this café is unable to accommodate you, try the Café Druzhba, the Friendship Café opposite. If time permits, an interesting antiquarian

The Alexander Column in Palace Square

bookshop to the left of the Literary Café, at 16 Nevsky Prospekt, is worth a browse.

After lunch, it's time to go and see the **Winter Palace** which houses one of the finest art collections in the world – **The State Hermitage Museum.** (Open 10am–6pm, closed Monday.) To get to the Hermitage, continue walking beside the Moika River until you come to the next bridge (Pevchesky or Chorister's bridge) and turn left into Palace Square. In the centre of the square stands the

Alexander Column, which was erected to the design of A de Montferrand, who also designed St Isaac's, to commemorate the victory of Russian armies in the Napoleonic War during the reign of Alexander I. This 47m (156ft) column is made from a granite monolith brought from the northern shore of the Gulf of Finland. On the south side of the square is the curved yellow General Staff building, designed by Rossi. The avocado green and gold building is the Hermitage.

The Hermitage became a museum under Catherine the Great and is made up of three buildings, the green Winter Palace, the Small Hermitage and the Large Hermitage. The Winter Palace which you see now is the fourth version. The architect was Rastrelli, and the work began in 1754 during Elizabeth's reign. It was the home of the Imperial family, with the exception of Paul I. The adjoining Small Hermitage was built as a retreat for Catherine, and was followed by the Large Hermitage.

If you do not want to spend all afternoon here, in the summer you can take a **boat trip** from just outside the entrance, which is on the other side of the building, facing the river. These last one hour and go up the Neva to one of the most beautiful buildings in the city – the Smolny Cathedral, considered by many to be Rastrelli's masterpiece.

There are many different estimates of how many years it would take to look round the Hermitage if you looked at every picture for so many seconds. So, for now, we will limit our tour to a few rooms of Western European art on the first floor.

Directly in front of the entrance are the ticket offices – KACCA. You will not be admitted if you are carrying large bags. They should be left in the cloakrooms to the right of the ticket offices. You will also be charged extra if you wish to take photographs. The entrance to the museum is to the left of the ticket offices through the Rastrelli gallery. You should now make your way to the side of the Winter Palace that looks onto Palace Square, to the first floor, to rooms 315–20 which contain the work of the French Impressionists and rooms 344–9 which house paintings by Picasso and Matisse. If you have time on your way out, there is a fascinating collection of primitive Russian culture and art on the ground floor (rooms 11–69).

If the Hermitage is closed I would suggest you retrace your steps back across the square to the River Moika, cross the bridge and turn left until you come to the **Pushkin Flat-Museum** at No 12. Pushkin is, deservedly, a cult figure in

Inside the Hermitage

Church of the Resurrection

this city and it would be almost sacrilegious not to pay a visit. (Open 10.30am–6pm, closed Tuesday.) 'Walkmans' are available with tapes in various languages. If you're interested in seeing what is on at the **Capella Music Hall** (Glinka Academic Choir) in the evenings, it's on the same side, at No 20, Naberezhnaya Moiki, by the bridge.

After a visit to the Hermitage, I suggest you try its café. The standard has definitely improved since the Soviet era.

The House of Scholars (turn right out of the Hermitage entrance and walk along the embankment to No 26) has its own café but it tends to open and close when it feels like it. Go in past the attendant's desk on the left and carry on straight up some steps. The setting, looking out across the river, is superb.

It would be hard to guess from the outside that inside is a wonderful café (roubles) with a beautiful view across the water. Go in through the main doors, past the attendant's desk on the left and carry straight on. You could not find a grander setting to have a tea or coffee in; they also serve alcoholic drinks.

Otherwise, take a taxi or any bus or trolleybus up the Nevsky Prospekt and alight at the second intersecting waterway, the Griboedova/Ekaterinsky Canal. Turn left

The Moika from Nevsky Prospekt

up the canal towards the onion-domed **Church of the Resurrection**, also known as the Church of the Saviour 'on the spilled blood'. Alexander II was mortally wounded on this spot. On your right at No 14 you will see a bar called **Chaika** – Seagull – a Russian-German joint venture where you can have a bar meal. Its style is that of a continental pub. If you want to settle in for a long session the Chaika is open until 3am.

The Tsars' City

Peter the Great's wooden cabin, the Peter and Paul Fortress, a walk along the shore, the Cruiser 'Aurora', the Summer Palace and the Russian Museum. Book Sadkos, Chopsticks or Restaurant Europe for dinner.

—Take the metro (or taxi) to Metro Station Gorkovskaya.—

As the Fortress does not open at the crack of dawn (11am–6pm, closed Wednesday and last Tuesday of the month) you have just the right amount of time to take a leisurely walk from the metro down to the river (600m/656yds) to see Peter the Great's **Wooden Cabin**. (Open 10am–6pm, closed Tuesday and last Monday of the month.) Come out of the metro, bear right, and with Kamenoostrovsky (Kirovsky) Prospekt in sight to your left, walk through the Alexandrinsky Gardens until you come to the river. Just before the bridge, turn left and walk along the river embankment. When you come to some steps on your right on which sit some sculpted oriental beasts, the Wooden Cabin is directly to your left in the trees. Although protected by stone on the outside, inside you will be able to see a perfectly preserved two-roomed hut, made out of rough pine in three days in 1703.

Now go back to the Fortress and enter through the main, St John's Gate. You are now on **Zayachy** or **Hare Island.** The day that the Fortress was built – 27 May 1703 – is considered to be the day that the town was founded. It was built by Peter the Great to defend the banks of the Neva from the Swedes and served as a fortress until the early 19th century when it became one of the most deathly prisons of Tsarist Russia, Russia's Bastille.

Buy your tickets at the KACCA on the right-hand side. There are various museums within the Fortress, but your ticket should enable you to enter them all. Of particular interest is the **Cathedral of St Peter and St Paul**. To get there come out of the ticket office and walk straight into the centre of the Fortress through the next (St Peter's) gate.

Peter and Paul Fortress, with Cathedral spire

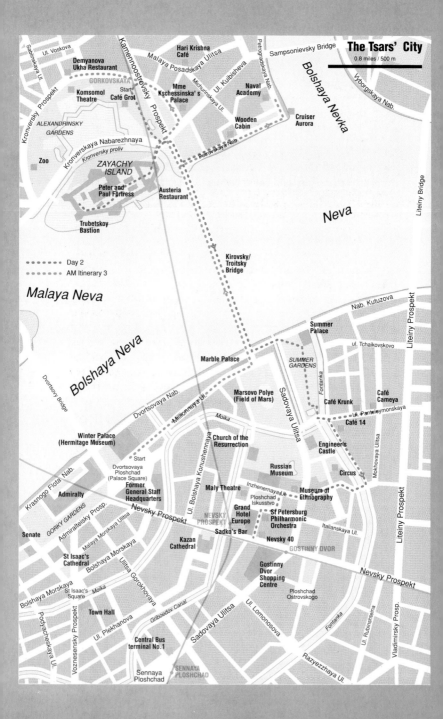

The Tsars' City

0.8 miles / 500 m

Bolshaya Nevka

Vyoorgskaya Nab.

Sampsonievsky Bridge

Liteiny Bridge

Neva

Ul. Voskova

Sabinskaya Ul.

Demyanova
Ukha Restaurant

Hari Krishna
Café

Malaya Posadskaya Ulitsa

Petrogradskaya Nab.

GORKOVSKAYA

Start
Café Grot

Mme
Kschessinska's
Palace

Ul. Kuibisheva

Michurinskaya Ul.

Naval
Academy

Cruiser
Aurora

Komsomol
Theatre

Kronversky Prospekt

Kamennoostrovsky Prospekt

Wooden
Cabin

ALEXANDRINSKY
GARDENS

Kronverskaya Nabarezhnaya

Kronversky proliv

Zoo

ZAYACHY
ISLAND

Petrovskaya Nab.

Peter and
Paul Fortress

Austeria
Restaurant

Trubetskoy
Bastion

Kirovsky/
Troitsky
Bridge

· · · · · Day 2
· · · · · AM Itinerary 3

Malaya Neva

Nab. Kutuzova

Liteiny Prospekt

Summer
Palace

ul. Tchaikovskovo

SUMMER
GARDENS

Bolshaya Neva

Marble Palace

Fontanka

Café Krunk

Café
Cameya

Dvortsovy Bridge

Dvortsovaya Nab.

Millionnaya Ul.

Marsovo Polye
(Field of Mars)

Sadovaya Ulitsa

Ul. Panteleymonskaya

Café 14

Molka

Winter Palace
(Hermitage Museum)

Church of the
Resurrection

Engineer's
Castle

Mokhovaya Ulitsa

Start

Dvortsovaya
Ploshchad
(Palace Square)

Russian
Museum

Circus

Krasnogo Flota Nab.

Former
General Staff
Headquarters

Ul. Bolshaya Konushennaya

Maly Theatre

Inzhenernaya Ul.

Museum of
Ethnography

Admiralty

GORKY GARDENS

Admiralteisky Prosp.

Nevsky Prospekt

Ploshchad
Iskusstvo

Grand
Hotel
Europe

St Petersburg
Philharmonic
Orchestra

Italianskaya Ul.

Liteiny Prospekt

Senate

NEVSKY
PROSPEKT

Sadko's Bar

Nevsky 40

St Isaac's
Cathedral

Kazan
Cathedral

Malaya Morskaya Ulitsa

GOSTINNY DVOR

Nevsky Prospekt

Bolshaya Morskaya

Ulitsa Gorokhovaya

Gostinny
Dvor
Shopping
Centre

Ploshchad
Ostrovskogo

St Isaac's
Square

Molka

Ul. Lomonosova

Fontanka

Ul. Rubshteina

Vladimirsky Prosp.

Bolshaya Morskaya

Town Hall

Podyacheskaya Ul.

Ul. Plekhanova

Griboedov Canal

Central Bus
terminal No.1

Sadovaya Ulitsa

Razyezzhaya Ul.

Voznesensky Prospekt

Sennaya
Ploshchad

SENNAYA
PLOSHCHAD

Inside the Cathedral

The yellow building of the cathedral will be obvious and it is from here that the famous spire rises. Inside you will see the tombs of most of the Russian emperors and empresses. Peter the Great lies in a white marble sarcophagus in front in the far right-hand corner. Monarchists will be proud to see that Vladimir Kirilovich, who was the nearest surviving relative to Nicholas II and who lived in exile in Paris, was recently buried here.

Also take a look at the prison cells in the **Trubetskoy Bastion**. To get there, turn left as you come out of the church and follow the path round beside a pale pink building. The entrance is in the yellow building on the corner. Peter the Great's son, Alexis, was murdered here in 1718. Dostoevsky served time here, as did Lenin's brother and both Trotsky and Gorky.

If you hear an unearthly sound at midday, it is only the Fortress' cannon going off. Foreigners will jump in fright whilst the people of St Petersburg merely check their watches.

Retrace your steps back to Gorkovskaya metro station. Just south of the metro in Alexandrinsky park is the Café Grot which is housed inside an artificial mound – 'Grot' means grotto in Russian. The nearby Hare Krishna café, at 2 Mala Posadskaya Ulitsa, serves vegetarian snacks and herbal tea.

Now cross Troitsky (Kirovsky) bridge, turning left when you get to the opposite embankment, Naberezhnaya Kutuzova. This is a ten-minute walk. If your legs are tired, take a bus or tram one stop over the bridge. Stop to admire the black and gold railings of the **Summer Gardens** to your right before you enter.

Fortress doors

In the Summer Gardens

The Summer Gardens is one of the finest parks in the city, full of statues and lime trees. In the northeast corner stands Peter's small **Summer Palace.** (Open 10am–6.30pm, closed Tuesday and last Monday of the month. Also closed October–May.) The palace, one of St Petersburg's first stone edifices, was built by Domenico Trezzini – whose works are typical of early Russian baroque – in 1712. Peter moved into his palace before the decorators had time to finish working on it and spent all his summers there from then on. The two-storey palace has a simple layout, but if you have enough time it is well worth a visit.

You are probably looking forward to lunch by now, so continue through the gardens as far as the pond. Exit after the urn statue through a gate bordered by double-headed eagles. Opposite you is

Pushkin stands outside the Russian Museum

the terracotta **Engineers' Castle** (open 10am–6pm, closed Tuesday) where Paul I was assassinated. The building has been under restoration but now houses some of the exhibits from the Russian Museum. Turn to the left, crossing over the Fontanka Canal, turn right and continue until you see a yellow sign for a café directly on the left. The entrance is under the arches. It is a very good, privately run rouble café which does not have a name, but is at **No 14**. Lots of fresh vegetables. You bag a table then order and pay at the counter. The menu is only in Russian, but persevere – someone will help translate. If it is closed, there are two alternatives. Standing with the café behind you, turn right along the Fontanka, taking the first right up Ulitsa Panteleymonskaya/Pestelya. The first road on the left, Solyannoe Pereulok, has the **Café Krunk** on the right-hand side, and the next street off Ulitsa Panteleymonskaya/Pestelya to the left, Ulitsa Furmanova, has the **Café Cameya** on the right-hand side at No 32.

After lunch walk along the Fontanka Canal with the Engineers' Castle on your right until you come to the next bridge. Turn right over the bridge into Inzheneryaya Ulitsa. Pass the **circus** on your right, (check out what's on and if they have tickets) then cross over Sadovaya Ulitsa. Keep walking until you reach Ploshchad Iskusstvo or Square of the Arts. **The Russian Museum** stands in the middle of the square to your right as you come in (10am–6pm, closed Tuesdays). Don't confuse it with the first museum you pass, the Museum of Ethnography.

The yellow classical building of the Russian Museum was built by Rossi between 1819–25 for Grand Duke Mikhail, the younger brother of Alexander I and Nicholas I. Unlike the Hermitage, it houses only Russian items and is a smaller, more manageable museum. The exhibits cover almost 1,000 years of the history of Russian art, including folk art, from an amazing icon collection to work of the present day. When repairs are being done, which is quite often, the pictures move rooms. Don't miss the icons or the paintings of the second half of the 19th century – particularly those of Repin (whose house is included elsewhere in this book), as well as the Russian art of the avant garde (Malevich, Filonov). And always watch out for the temporary exhibitions, for some of the finest contemporary art.

If you have time, or would prefer an option, next door lies the **Russian Ethnographical Museum**, also well worth a visit, even though the USSR has now become history. (Open 10am–6pm, closed Monday.) Children would find this much more amusing than the Russian Museum.

Whilst you are in Ploshchad Iskusstvo you may like to take the opportunity to check what is currently on at the **St Petersburg Philharmonic Orchestra** (2 Mikhailovskaya Ulitsa/Ulitsa Brodskovo), and at the **Maly** (Small) **Theatre of Opera and Ballet** (1 Ploshchad Isskustv). In the middle of the square stands a famous statue of Alexander Pushkin by one of the city's leading sculptors, Mikhail Anikuchin.

Cross over the square and with the Russian Museum directly behind you walk down Mikhailovskaya Ulitsa/Ulitsa Brodskovo. On the right is one of the city's most luxurious hotels, the **Grand Hotel Europe. Sadkos**, a hard currency bar and part of the hotel, has its own entrance on the right-hand side, after the main hotel entrance. You can also have just a drink inside the hotel itself. You can either eat at Sadkos, or Chopsticks (also inside the Grand Hotel Europe and suitable for vegetarians) or if you feel extravagant, try the hotel's Restaurant Europe

In the Grand Hotel Europe

DAY 3

Five Palaces

A Day in Tsarskoe Selo (Tsar's Village), previously called Detskoe Selo (Children's Village) and Pushkin, situated 25km (15½ miles) south of St Petersburg. The main Catherine Palace is closed on Tuesdays and the last Monday of the month. Take food and drink.

—Take the metro or a taxi to Pushkinskaya (Vitebsk Station) the starting point.—

There are five palaces situated near St Petersburg. Everyone has their favourite and it is impossible to recommend one more highly than the other. **Tsarskoe Selo** is well worth seeing because of its

Taking the train to the palaces

sheer splendour and opulence, and for that reason I have included it as a 'must-see' on your first three days. **Petrodvoretz** would normally be chosen in its place but, unfortunately it is undergoing extensive repairs to the front of the building although its insides are intact and open to the public. **Pavlovsk** is smaller and more understated and in that lies its great charm. It has been lovingly and painstakingly restored. The less well-known of the five are **Gatchino** and **Oranienbaum.** My favourite is Oranienbaum. The main palace there has not been restored yet but is of particular interest as it escaped the bombs of World War II. Gatchino has several rooms open to the public, but much work has still to be done. This palace has a beautiful stone exterior which changes colour with the sun and is far less ornate than the others.

I recommend you choose Tsarskoe Selo as the first palace to see and if possible that you go on a weekday when the trains are not so crowded and there will be fewer visitors to the palace. Try also to go on a fine day, so as not to miss the gardens.

As you come out of the metro station Pushkinskaya, you cannot miss the huge building of the **Vitebsk Railway Station.** To get to the ticket offices, you do not have to go into the main station building but, if you have time, take a look inside at the beautiful

Facade of the Catherine Palace

art nouveau interior. Vitebsk was the first Russian railway station and the line between here and Tsarskoe Selo was the first experimental railway (1837).

Walk round the main station building until you find the small ticket office which adjoins it. When buying your ticket ask for Detskoe Selo (or Pushkin if you can't pronounce the first), and a return ticket – *tooda i obratno*. The village has undergone various confusing name changes, Tsarskoe Selo – Detskoe Selo – Pushkin. The railway station is called Detskoe Selo, but if you say Pushkin, everyone knows what you mean.

Turn left out of the office and continue until you come to some double steps which lead onto the platforms. Trains depart regularly for Detskoe Selo and the name will be up on the platform. If you are in any doubt, just ask any Russian on the station, in whatever language.

Cupid in the Palace

Alight at the station and take bus No 371 or walk for 20 minutes, exploring the town as you go. Ask for *Dvoretz* or palace. You will know when you have arrived thanks to the bright turquoise and gold of the **Catherine Palace** shining through the trees.

Peter the Great's wife, Catherine, chose the site around 1718 to build a stone country house as a surprise for her husband while he was away for two years in Poland. It seems to be the fate of each royal palace to be altered by successive monarchs and Peter's daughter, the Empress Elizabeth, decided to improve on the country house when she came to the throne in 1741. She asked Rastrelli to design a royal residence modelled on Versailles and named it the Catherine Palace in honour of her mother.

Warming up for a recital

Although it was added to by subsequent rulers, particularly by Catherine the Great, whose architect, the Scotsman Charles Cameron, gave the palace a more stately feel, it is above all Elizabeth's creation. It was not finished in her lifetime, but the extravagant baroque design was symbolic of the mood which predominated during her reign.

There is another, smaller palace in the grounds, less ornate, more classical – the **Alexander Palace**, which was presented to Alexander I by his grandmother, also called Catherine, on the occasion of his marriage. It is not, however, open to the public, but well worth a look from the outside.

The town expanded rapidly in the late 19th and 20th centuries and it is said that Tsarskoe Selo was the first city with electric street lighting in Europe. It developed as a popular summer resort – the climate is much better here than in St Petersburg – and after the Revolution many of the houses of the nobility were turned into sanatoria and holiday homes for children. In 1918 it was renamed Detskoye Selo (Children's Village). The name

The Great Hall, Catherine Palace

changed again in 1937 to Pushkin as the great poet had studied at the Lycée in 1811, aged 12. In 1941 Tsarskoe Selo was occupied by the German army, which unfortunately left both the city and the palace in ruins. The Catherine Palace has undergone major restoration since that time.

For entry to the Catherine Palace, the KACCA is in the main part, the entrance on the 300-m (984-ft) facade that you face, with the park behind. You may find several tour groups going round – and if you want to find out the finer details of every room, it is well worth tagging on to one of these. You will be asked to wear *tapochki* – slippers which you tie on over your shoes to prevent damage to the floors, and they also help to polish them. In every room there will be a museum attendant, usually a *babushka* – which literally means old woman but has a wider connotation here. These formidable ladies can seem very fierce and are ready to tell you off as soon as opportunity permits.

One of the mysteries of this palace is the disappearance of the amber panels given to Peter the Great by Friedrich-Wilhelm, King of Prussia, in exchange for 248 soldiers, a lathe and a wine cup made by Peter himself. They disappeared after the German occupation. To this day, rumours abound that they have been found, but they *are* only rumours.

In the park of the Catherine Palace

The interior, like the exterior, is a mixture of different architects, different styles, the baroque of Rastrelli and the classicism of Cameron. **The Great Hall**, with its mirrors, wood carvings, glistening gold and feeling of space is perhaps the most sumptuous of all.

There is a great deal to see in the park and I would particularly recommend that you first walk away from the house, past the **Upper** and **Lower Baths** to the **Hermitage**, then round the great pond, in the direction of the Alexander Park and Palace, time permitting. Don't miss the Fountain of the Milkmaid with the broken pitcher, inspired by a La Fontaine fable, or the Caprice. Also make sure you see the courtyard side of the palace, with its impressive railings. When visiting a building that has been so highly restored, it is important at the same time to see the ruins – so take a look at the still-to-be restored **Chinese Village** on the way.

Morning Itineraries

1. The Kuznechny Market

The Vladimir Church, the Kuznechny Market, Dostoevsky's house and the museum of the Arctic and Antarctic. If you want to buy food at the market, take your own containers – plastic bags for fruit and vegetables, jars for honey and sour cream.

–Take the metro or a taxi to Metro Vladimirskaya/ Dostoevskaya.–

You will not starve if you go to the **Kuznechny Market**. It is well worth a visit, even if you don't wish to buy anything. You will pay more here than in the shops, but you will pay for quality and you

Quality produce is sold from the market stalls

Honey for sale

won't have to queue. If you are going out of town on a day trip, this is a very good place for you to buy your picnic.

Before you go into the market, visit the yellow **Vladimir Church** which you will see on your right as you come out of Vladimir metro. This is a functioning Russian Orthodox church and is open 9am–8pm. It is a mark of respect for women to cover their heads when they go in. No one knows who the architect was, although Quarenghi added the bell tower and Melnikov the classical hall in 1783 and 1831 respectively.

Turn left out of the church and continue to the left into Kuznechny Pereulok (small street). The streets will be lined with people selling their wares, but the actual market is in the covered building on the right, built during the Soviet period. You will be dazzled by the splendour of the display, particularly in the summer months. The produce is flown in from all over the republics as well as coming from nearby. The vegetables and fruit seem bigger and better than anywhere else. You will be invited to try many kinds of different honey, *tvorog* or curd cheese and *smetana* or sour cream, as well as to buy flowers. The market is not usually rife with pick-

The Market

0.8 miles / 500 m

Ul. Zhukovskogo
Liteiny Prosp.
Ul. Mayakovskogo
Ul. Vosstaniya
Nevsky Prospekt
PLOSHCHAD VOSSTANIYA
Vladimirsky Prosp.
MAYAKOVSKAYA
Nevsky Restaurant
Ploshchad Vosstaniya
Moscow Station
Vladimir Church
The Museum of the Arctic and Antarctic
Kuznechny Market
Start
Kuznechny Pereulok
VLADIMIRSKAYA/ DOSTOEVSKAYA
Dostoevsky's House
Ul. Dostoevskogo
Cafe Iveria
Marata
Pushkinskaya Ul.
Ligovsky Prospekt
Razyezzhaya Ul.
Ulitsa
Borovaya Ul.
Transportny Per.

Dostoevsky's study

pockets, but be careful all the same.

Turn right out of the market and walk up the street on the market side. Cross over the next small street and on the corner straight in front of you, in the basement, is the entrance to **Dostoevsky's House** (open 10.30am–6pm, closed Monday and last Wednesday of the month). Dostoevsky lived here from 1878 until his death on 28 January 1881 – at precisely 8.38pm, as the family clock records. When he died, his wife Anna Grigorievna arranged for a photographer to take pictures of his study, which proved invaluable when the house was restored.

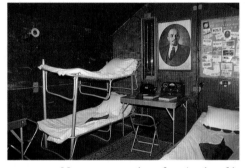

Although the furniture dates back to the time when Dostoevsky occupied the flat, it is not the original – but there are many of the author's personal belongings here, such as his hat. He wrote *The Brothers Karamazov* here; it was intended to be a trilogy, but he only completed the first book before his death.

Museum recreation of an Arctic cabin

Turn right out of Dostoevsky's house, continue up Kuznechny Pereulok, then take the next left turn into Ulitsa Marata. If you have time to kill before lunch, the **Museum of the Arctic and Antarctic** (open 10am–6pm, closed Monday and Tuesday) stands to your right, a huge cube-shaped building with a dome above it, which has amazing displays, documenting the various Russian expeditions to the polar regions.

There is a good Georgian café, the **Iveria** (roubles), at 35 Ulitsa Marat. From the Museum, turn left down Ulitsa Marat and look out for No 35 on the opposite side of the road and the sign for a café. Whilst I have always had good meals here, you can catch it on an off day. If you don't like the look of it then I suggest that you try the **Shakherezada Café** at 3 Razyeszhaya Pernelok (Arabian-Russian cuisine), or the large **Nevsky Restaurant**, situated on the corner of Ulitsa Marat and the Nevsky Prospekt. If you choose the Iveria, order their delicious bread *Pochahurie* as well as their *lobio* bean dish at the counter. Relax in a cheerful room that does not block out the daylight as do so many other Russian restaurants.

2. The Alexander Nevsky Lavra

Catherine the Great's Convent for the Education of Well-born Young Ladies and the Alexander Nevsky Monastery, built in the time of Peter the Great.

—Take a taxi to Smolny or metro to Chernyshevskaya followed by bus No 26 to Ploshchad Rastrelli. If you leave out Smolny, go by metro to Ploshchad Alexander Nevskovo.—

If you do not want to get up at the crack of dawn, I would suggest you limit this trip to the **Alexander Nevsky Lavra** only. If not, the **Smolny Cathedral** is one of the most breathtakingly beautiful buildings in the city and can be seen on the way. A former museum, it is now used for concerts. (If you're interested, find out about tickets inside.) You may have seen it against the skyline. Painted pale blue and white, in the shape of a Greek cross, it seems to float rather than stand on the horizon.

Smolny means tar and it seems somewhat incongruous that the site of such a cathedral was a tar yard until 1723, when it was moved to another location. Elizabeth decided to build a convent there in 1744 and hired Rastrelli, who never in fact finished the job – it was completed by the architect V P Stasov, who added several new structures between1832–35 during Catherine's reign, and became an institute 'for the education of well-born young ladies', the first of its kind in Russia.

At the beginning of the next century the **Smolny Institute** moved to the yellow, classical building next door, designed by Quarenghi. This was to become the headquarters of the Bolshevik Central Committee, and it was from here that Lenin led the uprising in October 1917 that ended the Tsarist rule.

The **Alexander Nevsky Lavra** is situated on **Ploshchad Alexan-**

The Smolny Cathedral

Alexander Nevsky Lavra

dra Nevskovo, just opposite the metro station of the same name. From Smolny, take a taxi to **Ploshchad Alexandra Nevskovo** or ask for the hotel Moskva. If you want to go by public transport, bus No 26 from Smolnaya Ulitsa should take you all the way to Ploshchad Alexandra Nevskovo. You will know you are there when you see the **Hotel Moskva** (Moscow).

Coming by metro you will find the Hotel Moskva where you can stop for a coffee right next door to the metro exit. You will also see the yellow archway into the *lavra* on the other side of the square opposite.

The **Alexander Nevsky Lavra** is the oldest and most beautiful monastery complex in the city, named after the Russian prince who saved the city from the Swedes in the 13th century and was canonised after his death. His remains were brought here in a silver coffin – which was then moved to the Hermitage. It is important to remember to visit in the morning because in the afternoon between 2–5pm the **Holy Trinity cathedral** is closed for cleaning.

If you are not interested in looking at gravestones all morning you can still enjoy the surroundings, as well as the peace and quiet. It is perfectly acceptable to walk into the church when a service is being held and many people seem to come and go in this way, even worshippers. And don't be surprised if you see a baptism, a wedding and an open coffin all in one morning.

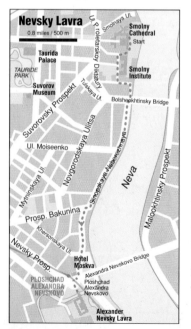

Lavra is a title bestowed upon a monastery of the highest order, the seat of Metropolitans, and before the Revolution there were only four in Russia – Kievo-Pecherskaya, Troitse-Sergieva (in Moscow), Pochayevskaya and the Alexander Nevsky. The Alexander Nevsky became a *lavra* in 1797 although it was founded by Peter the Great in 1713 – his sister Natalya Alexeyevna is buried here. The monastery was enlarged under Peter's successors, and the Holy Trinity Cathedral was built in Catherine's time by architect Vasily Stasov.

The *lavra* is still a burial ground for famous people – 'there's a long queue' I was told by one of the at-

Tchaikovsky's tomb in Tikhvin Cemetery

tendants. Recently, Anna Akhmatova's son, Lev Gumilev, was buried here, as was Georgy Tovstonogov, one of the most famous contemporary theatre directors. There are several cemeteries inside the complex. Some interesting headstones can be seen in the central courtyard, outside the cathedral, among them is the propeller of an aeroplane which marks the grave of a pilot who was killed in World War II.

Most interesting of all are the two cemeteries, the **Tikhvin** and the **Lazarus**, which lie directly to the left and right of the gates as you enter the monastery. You have to pay to enter and tickets are sold at the gates. To the left is the Lazarus Cemetery where Peter's sister is buried. There are also many important architects buried here, such as Giacomo Quarenghi (the Manege, the Hermitage Theatre), Andreyan Zakharov (the Admiralty), Carlo Rossi (Russian Museum, General Staff Headquarters in Palace Square and the Alexandrinsky Theatre) and Andrei Voronikhin (the Kazan Cathedral).

To your right is the Tikhvin Cemetery where famous composers lie buried, such as Mikhail Glinka, Pyotr Tchaikovsky, Modest Mussorgsky, Nikolai Rimsky-Korsakov. Here also lies Fyodor Dostoevsky and the sculptor Pyotr Klodt, who created the horses on the Anichkov Bridge.

The **Museum of Town Sculpture** has recently been undergoing extensive repairs. But if it is open and running (open 11am–7pm, closed Thursday and last Tuesday of the month), it can be found housed inside the **Church of the Annunciation**, to the left of the main entrance, which was built in 1717–22 by Domenico Trezzini.

General Suvorov, Imperial Russia's most prominent military leader, is buried here. And the beautiful **Holy Trinity Cathedral** (1778–90, by Ivan Starov) is inside the main complex with the Metropolitan's House situated opposite.

The *lavra* is unfortunately not within easy walking distance of restaurants, but for lunch why not try Russian snacks at 11 Sergeya, 172 Nevsky Prospekt. For ease, though not such a good meal, you could simply cross the road to the Hotel Moskva.

In the Church of the Annunciation

3. The Cruiser Aurora

The Marble Palace, the battleship 'Aurora' and Kschesshinska's Palace. Lunch at Demyanova Ukha, or the Victory. Book a table, see the map on page 28 for the route.

–Take a taxi to Palace Square or metro to Nevsky Prospekt.–

The **Marble Palace** (Mramorny Dvoretz) is situated near the Field of Mars (Marsovo Polye). It is well worth a visit, if you do not mind a twenty-minute walk over **Troitsky** (Kirovsky) Bridge to the cruiser *Aurora* afterwards. If however you do not have a great deal of time, start at the *Aurora*.

The entrance to the Marble Palace is at 5, Ulitsa Millionnaya – Millionaires' Row. Until recently the street was known as Ulitsa Khalturina after S N Khalturin who planted a bomb inside the Winter Palace in 1880. The old pre-Revolutionary street name has now been reinstated, however, so the city can once again boast a Millionaires' Row.

Walk up Ulitsa Khalturina from Palace Square – it runs behind the Hermitage Buildings (look out for the Atlantes that support the porch of the New Hermitage building, designed by the 19th-century German architect Leo von Klenze). The walk is about 800m (875 yds), ending before the Field of Mars. The grey facade of the palace is to your left in a courtyard.

The Aurora is moored by the Naval Academy

The Marble Palace was built by Catherine the Great for her favourite, Grigory Orlov, who died before it was completed. The architect was Antonio Rinaldi. It was lived in by a Grand Duke before the Revolution, and in 1937 it became a Lenin Museum. Now it is part of the Russian Museum and holds various temporary exhibitions. It can look somewhat austere from the outside, but do look inside, even if you are not going to see an exhibition there – the interior is wonderfully extravagant.

Now walk across the Troitsky (Kirovsky) Bridge, turn right and proceed along the embankment, past Peter the Great's wooden house, until you come to the point where the river divides to the left into the Bolshaya Neva. This is where the *Aurora* is moored, in front of the blue, baroque **Nakhimov Naval Academy**. (The *Aurora* is open 10.30am–5pm, closed on Friday.)

Old Soviet leaflets on the *Aurora* write proudly of how the ship 'heralded a new era in the history of mankind', how it was awarded the Order of the Red Banner of Honour in 1924 etc. On 25

October 1917 at 9.45pm the *Aurora* fired a blank round – a signal for the insurgent forces to storm the Winter Palace, the seat of the Provisional Government – and thereby became a symbol of the Revolution. It now lies 'at its eternal anchorage'. The *Aurora* also served the Tsarist government back in 1904-5 at Tsu-Shima, just after it was built, and now flies the Tsarist flag. And it remains very well maintained, scrubbed and polished to this day.

Walk back along the embankment, the way you came, turn right when you come to the Troitsky (Kirovsky) Bridge, and walk down Kamenoostrovsky (Kirovsky Prospekt) with the Peter and Paul Fortress to your left. Turn right up Ulitsa Kuibisheva and at No 4, where it intersects with Kronversky Prospekt (Prospekt Maxim Gorkovo), is what was the Museum of the October Revolution, now called the **Museum of the Political History of Russia**.

This building is where the ballerina Mathilde Kschessinska lived. Kschessinska, one of the leading ballerinas at the turn of the century, made her debut at the Mariinsky (Kirov) Theatre. She is also known to have had an affair with Nicholas II, before he became Tsar. The house, built in the Style Moderne by A I Gogen, was a centre for St Petersburg society. In 1917 it was used as the Bolshevik Party headquarters and Lenin delivered speeches from the balcony, particularly his famous 'April Theses'. Look out for the amazing stained glass windows, which would not have been there in Kschessinska's time.

In the Revolution Museum

For lunch I would particularly recommend a fish restaurant on 53 Kronvesky Prospekt called **Demyanova Ukha** – Demyan's Fish Soup – a 10-minute walk from here. The menu may be in Russian only, but persevere, it's worth it. If you find yourself completely stuck, ask for the soup – *ukha* or *Seeg* – salmon-like fish, and you can't go wrong with *ikra*, caviar. The restaurant is refreshingly simple in its log-cabin decor, and is very good.

If you fail to get in to Demyanova Ukha (and sometimes you have to knock very hard on the locked entrance door) try the Russian/German Victory Restaurant at 24 Kamenoostrovsky Prospekt.

The Sphinxes, Menshikov Palace, the Kunstkamera and a choice of places for lunch.

—Taxi to Most Lieutenant Schmidt (Vasilievsky Island side) or take the trolley bus No 10 north from Nevsky Prospekt, or the metro to Vasileostrovskaya, followed by bus Nos 6 or 47.—

This walk begins on Vasilievsky Ostrov (Island) by the statues of the **Egyptian Sphinxes** on Universitetskaya Naberezhnaya – University Embankment. The streets in this part of town are marked scientifically, divided up into lines, in honour of the scientist D I Mendeleyev, inventor of the periodic table, who worked in the building of the Twelve Colleges.

Inside the Menshikov Palace

The Sphinxes go back a long way – they date from the 13th century BC and were brought from Thebes in 1832. The long granite pier on which they stand is directly in front of the austere **Academy of Arts** (open 11am–7pm, closed Monday and Tuesday), created in 1757.

With the river to your right, walk past the **Obelisk** which commemorates the Russian victories over the Turks under the 18th-century Russian Field Marshal, Rumyantsev, and the next building is the famous **Menshikov Palace**, one of the city's first stone residences, built in the time of Peter the Great.

Alexander Menshikov was a life long friend, rival (he built splendid palaces) and sometimes enemy of Peter the Great. He was the city's first governor-general and head of the military department. Peter gave him Vasilievsky Island in 1707, and luckily he built the palace before Peter took back his present in 1714. The palace was used for entertaining guests before Peter built his own palaces. A look inside is recommended, as this is one of the few buildings whose early interior is still intact. (Open 10.30am–4.30pm, closed Monday.) To book a tour in your own language, call 213 1112.

Come out of the Menshikov Palace and turn left, past two 18th-century buildings, until you come to the terracotta red building of what is now part of **St Petersburg University**, called the Twelve Colleges. This is only a corner of the building, which stretches to your left down Mendeleyevskaya Linia. Again, it is one of the oldest in the city, first built by Peter the Great to house his *Kollegia* or ministries. Its construction was set as a competition – Russia's first. If you want to have a look inside, I doubt if anyone will turn you out; the entrance is on Mendeleyevskaya Linia.

Back on the Universitetskaya Naberezhnaya, the next building is the Academy of Sciences – created when the building next door, the

Prow on a pillar

Kunstkamera, became too crowded. For a further insight into the man who built this town, go and look at his Chamber of Curiosities in the **Kunstkamera – Museum of Anthropology and Ethnography in the name of Peter the Great** (the blue and white building with the tower). To book a tour in advance call 218 1413. The entrance is down the side street before the main building to your left, Tamozhenny Pereulok. The 'curiosities' include embryos and human organs, on the ground floor under the dome (open 11am–6pm, closed Friday, Saturday and the last Thursday in the month). It also houses the museum of the Russian scholar Mikhail Lomonosov (1711–65).

With the Kunstkamera behind you, follow the embankment until you come to the main road, with the Dvortsovy (Palace) Bridge on your right. Turn left and keep walking with the two **rostral columns** now in sight. The magnificent building which dominates the 'spit' is now the **Central Naval Museum** – before the Revolution it was the Stock Exchange. Until the 1880s this point of Vasilievsky Island was St Petersburg's main port. The red pillars were the light signals. They are decorated with the prows of boats which represent four great Russian rivers – the Volga, Dnieper, Neva and Volkhov.

If you have time, walk round the spit of the island where you will often see newlyweds drinking champagne and being photographed.

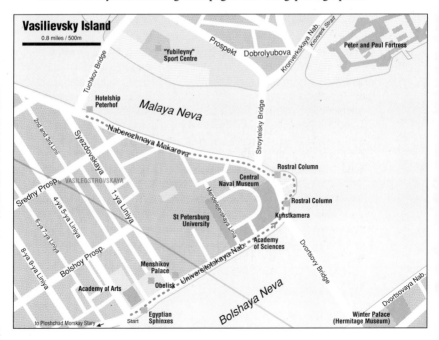

Newlyweds on the Spit

Apart from that, the view from the tip of the point is said to be one of the finest in the city.

Continue along the Makarov embankment with the Malaya Neva on your right-hand side; just before reaching the Tuchkov Bridge, you will find at anchor the Swiss-joint venture, **Hotelship Peterhof**. To see a bit more of Vasilevsky Island, take bus No 10 on Universitetksaya Naherezhnaya to Ploshcad Myorskoy Slavy where you can eat inside the Olympia Hotel. A shuttle bus leaves the Olympia on the hour which will take you as to the Grand Hotel Europe on Nevsky Prospekt after your lunch. Trolleybus 10 will also take you back up the Nevsky Prospekt.

Afternoon Itineraries

5. Up the Nevsky to the Anichkov Bridge

Ice-creams, market stalls, the Kazan Cathedral and the art nouveau House of Books. Lunch at the Café 01.

–Taxi to Admiralteistvo, or metro to Nevsky Prospekt, followed by bus No 7 to Palace Square. Nevsky Prospekt is 4.5km (2½ miles) long. This walk covers the first 2km (1 mile).–

Where you now stand – at the beginning of the **Nevsky Prospekt** with the **Admiralty** and **Palace Square** behind you – there once stood a forest. After the Admiralty was built in 1705, a path had to be cleared through it to link the ship-building yard with the town of Novgorod. People began to build houses and palaces along it, and called it the Nevsky Prospect. To this day it is the most important main street of the city.

At the beginning, the Nevsky seems like any old street, but as you keep walking it widens and to your right and left huge squares open out giving it a sense of space. It is also 'aired' by three waterways, the **Moika**, the **Griboedova** (Ekaterinsky) and the **Fontanka**.

The Nevsky is famous for ice-creams. You can buy them from kiosks on the street – the best ones are in wafer tubs and the prices vary according to their flavour, which is usually vanilla, but you sometimes find 'crême brulée' or a fruit flavour. Some visitors prefer Russian ice-creams for their home-made flavour, others will choose to go for the more Western varieties – and there are often queues outside a kiosk selling 'Princess'. It doesn't matter about the time of year – they taste just as good in the snow.

Stroganov Palace

Many of the St Petersburg streets are changing their names to previous versions, and often a pre-Revolutionary map is of more use to the present day visitor. The first important street you come to on your right will be **Malaya Morskaya Ulitsa** which was previously named Ulitsa Gogolya after the writer Gogol, who lived at No 17. Don't be alarmed that Tchaikovsky died at No 8 from drinking unboiled St Petersburg water. The next crossroads is the once fashionable **Bolshaya Morskaya Ulitsa** (Ulitsa Gertsena), home of the famous Fabergé shop (No 24, to the right). It is still a jeweller's shop, but unfortunately has lost its former glory.

The first river you come to is the **Moika** and on the right-hand side after the bridge stands the green and white **Stroganov Palace**. After the Palace, walk past **Bolshaya Konushennaya Ulitsa** (Ulitsa Zhelyabova), on your left, where Turgenev, and later on Nijinsky, lived at No 13. Rimsky-Korsakov lived at No 11. Further on to the right you will see the huge **Kazan Cathedral** with its 96 columns designed by the architect Andrei Voronikhin during and after the reign of Paul I. In the square in front of it are statues of the heroes of the 1812 war, M I Kutuzov and M B Barklay de Tolly. Once the Museum of the History of Religion and Atheism, it is now just the

Museum of Religion, has had its cross put back on top, and holds religious services. The entrance is on the Canal Griboedov/Ekaterinsky (open 11am–5pm, closed Tuesday). They hire out 'walkmans' so that you can listen to the tour in your own language.

Opposite at No 28 is the art nouveau **Dom Knigi**, House of Books, once the Singer sewing machine factory. It has a huge globe on the roof which can be seen from quite a distance. Try going up to the second floor, where you can often buy interesting maps and posters. As you turn left out of here and cross the bridge over the **Griboedova/Ekaterinsky**

Down Nevsky Prospekt

A Klodt horse, Anichkov Bridge

canal you see to your left the multi-coloured domes of the **Church of the Resurrection** built on the spot where Alexander II was assassinated. This church has been under restoration for some 25 years and has now emerged from its cocoon. Further up the Nevsky on the left-hand side, on the corner of Mikhail-ovskaya Ulitsa (Ulitsa Brod-skovo), is the yellow facade of the **Grand Hotel Europe**. This is now the most luxurious ho-tel in the city, but like the As-toria Hotel, its beautiful inte-rior structure was demolished to be replaced by a more vulgar, glitzy alternative. Mikhailovskaya Ulitsa/Ulitsa Brodskovo leads into **Ploshchad Iskusstv**, home of the Russian Museum.

You could stop at the Grand Hotel Europe for coffee or tea if you haven't been in already (entrance on Mikhailovskaya Ulitsa), and I would suggest the bar to your left as you go in (hard currency), or the hard currency bar **Sadkos**, part of the hotel, which has its own entrance after the corner of Mikhailovskaya Ulitsa and the Nevsky Prospekt. If it is after midday, there is a coffee shop a few metres up from the Grand Hotel Europe called **Nevsky 40** (hard currency, open noon–midnight). There are many coffee shops on Nevsky, but it is often hard to find a good one. For this reason, the places I have just mentioned, also recommended in *Day 2*, be-come something of a safe haven – comfort guaranteed. The yellow **Gostinny Dvor** facade is opposite you. This department store is well worth a visit and the discerning eye can find all sorts of curiosities to buy, although this may not seem apparent at first glance.

As you leave Gostinny Dvor you will pass through an underpass, opposite which at No 56 is a once-famous food shop called **Elyseevs**. Elyseev was a rich merchant and the extravagance of his design then parallels that of the Grand Hotel Europe now. Well worth a look.

On your right is a huge square with a statue of Catherine the Great and all her suitors. This is **Ploshchad Ostrovskovo**, laid out by the architect Rossi in the 1820s and 30s. Ostrovsky (1823–86) was a playwright who wrote about the bourgeoisie. Take a little de-tour here and walk through the square, where you may see men playing chess. To your right is the **Saltykov-Shchedrin Library**. You will see the **Pushkin Theatre of Drama** with its white columns through the trees, known more familiarly as the Alexandrinsky. Be-hind it, on the left-hand corner of the square and Rossi Street stands the **Museum of Theatrical and Musical Art** (open 11am–6pm, Wednesday 1pm–7pm, closed Tuesday and the last Friday of the month). As you come out of here, turn left, then left again

In Ploshchad Ostrovskovo

down **Teatralnaya Ulitsa**, previously called Ulitsa Zodchevo Rossi – street of the Master Builder Rossi with its perfect proportions; the width of the street equals the width of the buildings. Rossi designed many yellow buildings in the city, such as the General Staff headquarters in Palace Square and the Russian Museum (Mikhailovsky Palace). After all his work, he died relatively unknown and was only recognised posthumously.

On the left-hand side of this street is the **Vaganova Ballet School** where many famous Russian dancers trained, including Pavlova, Nijinsky, and, much later, Nureyev, Makarova and Baryshnikov. Now go back to the Nevsky and, keeping to the right-hand side, walk until you see the **Anichkov Bridge** with the dark red **Beloselsky-Belozersky Palace** behind.

The horses which decorate the Anichkov Bridge were designed by the sculptor Klodt. His initial plan for the bridge, four groups of horses, two of them identical, was never realised as Nicholas I kept giving one of each pair away – first to the king of Prussia and then to the king of Naples. Luckily, Klodt's further plan to prepare two new sculptures was accepted, and thus there are the four differing statues that we see today.

A good rouble restaurant for lunch can be found in Karavannaya (Ulitsa Tolmacheva). You will have to turn back the way you came, keeping to the same side of the Nevsky as the Lancôme shop. Turn right up Karavannaya when you get to Lancôme and keep walking until you see **Cafe 01** on the left-hand side at No 5.

If you have difficulty getting in, try the Aurora café at 58 Nevsky Prospekt or cross back over the Fontanka and try the café opposite at No 45 on the corner of Ulitsa Rubinshteina.

Elegant interior at Elyseev's

6. An Afternoon in Pavlovsk

A visit to Tsar Paul's palace and its huge gardens. The main palace is closed on Friday and the first Monday of the month. On Thursday many of the main rooms are closed. The КАССА is open 10am–5pm.

–Metro station Pushkinskaya, Vitebsk Railway Station to Pavlovsk Railway Station. Pavlovsk is situated 29km (18 miles) south of St Petersburg.–

As Pavlovsk is the smallest of the palaces, it is the best one to visit in the afternoon, after an early lunch or in combination with a visit to Tsarskoe Selo (see *Day 3*). It is a five-minute train journey from Detskoe Selo station and the main palace can be reached on foot from Pavlovsk Railway Station. (A 20-minute walk through the park gates directly opposite the station. Pay as you go in.) You can also take bus Nos 370, 383, 383(A) or 493 from outside Pavlovsk station.

Charles Cameron was the architect chosen to build the palace at Pavlovsk for Catherine the Great's son Paul and his wife Maria Feodorovna, as well as to re-design the gardens in the then fashionable English style. Later on the Italian Brenna was brought in. The land had originally been chosen for the royal hunt, because of all the elk and wild fowl. Unlike the other palaces, Pavlovsk is surrounded by small hills, through which flows the river Slavyanka. It is less extravagant, more classical in its design than the earlier palaces.

In time, the militaristic Paul transferred his affections to Gatchino where he had more space to drill his soldiers. Pavlovsk became his wife's favourite haunt. Paul lived in fear of conspirators. Stories abound of his petulant behaviour, his unfortunate looks, his paranoia.

In Pavlovsk park

Until 1915, Pavlovsk was lived in by the Tsars. During the first months of World War II, many of the valuable treasures were taken away or hidden. In 1944 the Germans set fire to the palace and the park was devastated as thousands of trees were cut down. Since then many have been re-

The Palace, Pavlovsk

Peace after hard sightseeing

planted and the restoration work to the building has just about been completed. Of all the palaces, Pavlovsk has been the most meticulously and lovingly restored. As you walk through you find yourself thinking back to the days when the palace was first built, wondering just how much the new work resembles the old. And it must be true to say that the shinier and glitzier it is, the more faithful it must be to the original.

There are usually groups of people being shown round by a tour guide. If you are lucky, you may be able to tag on to one that speaks your own language.

The rooms inside the palace, of which the finest are those up-stairs, reflect a combination of the styles of their various architects – Cameron, Brenna, Quarenghi, Rossi and Voronikhin. Paul's own character comes across in the **Hall of War** as well as the **Throne Room** and the **Hall of the Maltese Knights of St John**. His wife's **Hall of Peace** forms a pleasant and intended contrast. Look out for the tapestries in the Carpet Room which represent motifs from Cervantes' novel *Don Quixote* as well as for the French furniture (Henri Jacob), the embroidered French curtains in the **Greek Hall**, and in the Hall of Peace the tripod-vase of crystal and red-gold made in the St Petersburg glass factory in 1811. Also note the piano from London in Maria's boudoir, the Sèvres porcelain, and the statue of The Vestal Bearing Sacrifice (Louis Simon Boizot) in the **Ladies-in-Waiting's room** and the clock in Paul's study given to him by Pope Pius VI.

The gardens are very big indeed (600ha/1,482 acres), so keep to the pavilions nearer the palace such as the **Temple of Friendship**, intended to mark the friendship between Maria and her mother-in-law, the **Centaur Bridge**, the **Cold Baths**, the **Apollo Colonnade** and the **Pavilion of the Three Graces**. Or forget about the culture, sit back on a bench and enjoy the peaceful surroundings. The exit on to Ulitsa Revolutsi from where you take the bus back to the station is near here. Ask first for *autobus* and then for *Vokzal* which means station.

7. Piskarovskoye Memorial Cemetery

The cemetery for the victims of the Leningrad Blockade. For an early dinner on the way home, book at either the Tête à Tête or the Imperial (see Eating Out for details).

−Taxi to Piskarovskoye Kladbische or metro to Ploshchad Muzhestva; bus No 123 from Prospekt Nepokoryonnykh (Avenue of the Unvanquished).−

If you arrived in St Petersburg by air, you will have passed the impressive monument to the **Heroes of the defence of Leningrad** during World War II, in Ploshchad Pobedy − Victory Square − on the way in from the airport. Another, perhaps more important tribute is the **Piskarovskoye Memorial Cemetery.** Situated on the outskirts of the city amongst the new residential areas, it is not easy to reach by public transport and I'd advise taking a taxi. Although a visit to a cemetery may seem like a grim day out, I would highly recommend it as a fascinating record of a unique and devastating part of the city's history. In the past the experience seemed almost overbearing, as grim music played across the cemetery from loudspeakers. Thankfully this has now stopped, and you can wander peacefully without feeling emotionally blackmailed.

The Germans invaded Russia in July 1941 and reached Leningrad in August of that year. The city was encircled and completely cut off by road and by rail from September, when mass bombing began. Only a tiny tract of land on the shores of Lake Ladoga remained unoccupied by the enemy. When the narrower part of the lake froze up, a 37-km (23-mile) ice road − the Road of Life − was laid. But this did not provide enough food for an entire city and by November, the threat of mass famine was a real one. The bread ration at that time was 250g (9oz) a day for a worker, 125g (4½oz) for others. By November there was no electricity, and in December no water supply or public transport.

Soviet troops broke through the blockade in January 1943 and provisions reached the city through the Finland Station. The Germans were finally defeated in the Leningrad region in January 1944. During this time, some 16,000 civilians had been killed by air raids and shelling, and over 33,000 had been wounded. Hundreds of thousands more lives were lost through hunger. But during this time nothing came to a complete standstill. Everyone carried on working − factory workers continued to supply new and repaired tanks

Piskarovskoye

and ammunition, scientists researched new explosives from natural resources, Vavilov's famous Plant Breeding Institute remained intact – musicians even went on composing. Dmitri Shostakovich's Seventh (Leningrad) Symphony was broadcast on all wavelengths in 1942 from the Leningrad Philharmonia in Ploshchad Isskustvo. Gunfire and explosions could be heard in the background. Leningrad was awarded the order of Lenin in January 1945, for the outstanding services of its people to the country.

Four hundred and seventy thousand (yes, 470,000) victims of the blockade are buried in mass graves at Piskarovskoye on either side of the long central alley. Civilian graves are marked by a hammer and sickle, military ones by a star. On each mound is stamped the year that they died. On the wall behind the statue of the motherland is inscribed a poem by Olga Bergholtz, a Soviet poetess who worked throughout the siege on Radio Leningrad – part of it translates as '...here are townspeople – men women and children, Beside them are the soldiers of the Red Army...With their whole lives they defended you, Leningrad, Cradle of the Revolution. We cannot give here each of their noble names, There are so many under the granite...Everyone rose up as one saying we would sooner frighten death than let death frighten us.'

Don't miss the two rooms to the left and right of the entrance which chart the history of the siege, step by step, with excellent black and white photographic evidence and the famous document of a young girl's diary – each entry records the death of another member of her family, ending with the words 'They have all died'.

You should be able to catch a taxi back from just outside the cemetery gates. If you have time to spare, ask to be taken to **Workers' Island**, now called **Kamenny Ostrov** (stone island) on the way back. This is one of the three Kirov Islands and is a traditional sanatorium or *dacha* area, only about 1km (½ mile) in length. Nearby, across Ushakovsky Bridge, lies Chernaya Rechka metro station to your left. If you want to go straight to a restaurant for dinner, try either the excellent **Imperial** or **Tête à Tête restaurants.**

8. Moika Boat Trip and Baths

A sightseeing trip where you can plan your own route, and a visit to a traditional steam bath.

–Metro to Nevsky Prospekt. Trips (summer only) start where the Nevsky Prospekt crosses over the Moika Canal – at the Narodny or People's Bridge.–

Two kinds of boats go up the canals – the long river boats which seat many passengers and the smaller taxi-boats which seat up to 10 people. We are going to catch a taxi-boat. You will see signs for these on the Nevsky Prospekt as it crosses over the river Moika. These boats literally do operate as taxis so you have to catch one when it is free. The tours are obviously more popular in the summer months, and cannot run in the winter

Water taxi

when the canals freeze up, but there is no fixed time in the year that they start or stop – everything depends on the weather. Unlike on the large river boats, you will be charged in dollars. It is impossible to give an approximate price – the boatman will suggest a price which will probably sound too much so it is worth bargaining. Pay what you would think reasonable in Europe remembering that each tour lasts one hour, and that this is one of the best and most re-

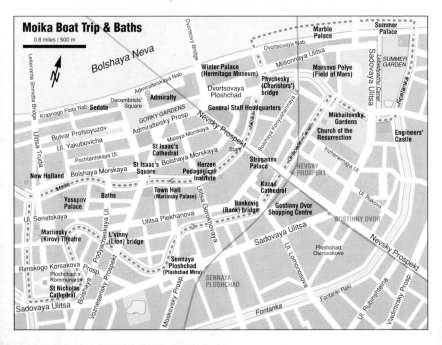

A quiet backwater

laxing ways to see the city.

The taxi-boats do not have a fixed route, so you can show the boatman the way you want to go by pointing at a map. (He will have one, but you may like to take your own just in case.) I would suggest the following – Moika River to New Holland, Kriukov Canal, Griboedova/Ekaterinsky Canal, join the Fontanka by the Summer Gardens, out into the Neva, turn left until the Hermitage where you turn left into a canal which takes you back to the Moika.

It is impossible to name each building that you pass or each bridge you go under, but look out for the following: the first building on your left after the Nevsky crosses the Moika is the green and white **Stroganov Palace**. Further on to the left is a former orphanage at No 48, now one of the buildings forming the **Herzen Pedagogical Institute**. Count one bridge and you then approach **St Isaac's Square** and the Statue of Nicholas I. To your left is the **Mariinsky Palace**, built in 1839–40 by A Stankenshneider, and presented by Nicholas I to his daughter Maria. It is now used as the city hall, the office of the mayor, and was heavily defended by barricades and crowds during the August 1991 abortive coup against Gorbachev's government. The bridge under which you pass at this point, the Blue Bridge (its original colour when it was wooden) is the widest in the city.

Further along on the left at No 94 stands the **Yusupov Palace**, home of the chief assassin of Rasputin, who was murdered here in 1916. This museum is highly recommended for a visit another time. Further on the right, where the boat will turn to the left up the Kriukov Canal, is the red brick of **New Holland**, where Peter the Great stored his shipbuilding timber. The next important building on the left is the pale green of the **Mariinsky (former Kirov) Theatre**, which backs onto the river. Maria, from whom the theatre takes its name, was the mother of Alexander II.

You will not be able to miss the sparkling domes of the **St Nicholas' or Sailors' Cathedral**, first the bell tower by the river, and then as you turn the corner

Down Griboedova Canal

into the Griboedova/Ekaterinsky Canal, the church itself. It was built between 1753-62 by S I Chevakinsky. The canal bends round and you go under the **L'vinny – Lion Bridge**. When the canal forms its next bend, to your right is famous Dostoevsky country. **Sennaya Ploshchad/Ploshchad Mira**, the former Haymarket, was an important setting in *Crime and Punishment*. Further on is another spectacular bridge – **Bank Bridge** – on which sit some sculpted griffins. According to ancient Greek mythology, griffins guard gold – and here they stand guard over the former State Bank which is located directly to the right.

Immediately afterwards comes the **Kazan Cathedral** and you now

The domes of St Nicholas

pass under the Nevsky Prospekt again, heading for the onion-domed church at the end of the canal, the **Church of the Resurrection**. Before you come to this, to your right is the yellow Benois Wing of the Russian Museum. You can now see the church close to, in all its splendour. After the church, you should bear right, with the **Field of Mars** on your left, and the **Mik-hailovsky (Russian Museum) Gardens** on your right. The next splendid sight you will see is the terracotta-red **Engineers' Castle** which looks more like a fortress. Here, Paul I was assassinated. Some 20 years later it became a Military Engineering Academy. The entrance to the Summer Gardens is just opposite it. You now come to the Fontanka canal and take a left towards what seems like the open sea. Just before you come to the Neva, the small yellow house to your left is Peter the Great's **Summer Palace**.

The boat should turn left past the gates to the Summer Gardens. Go under Troitsky (Kirovsky) Bridge with the Field of Mars to the left and the statue of the great General Suvorov, a hero of the campaign against Napoleon. The Field of Mars, a former marsh, then parade ground, was redesigned after the Revolution by the architect L V Rudnev. Many of the dead from the Revolution and Civil War are buried here and an eternal flame burns in the centre. Directly after this is the **Marble Palace**. You now have an incredible view of the city, which seems to be almost floating on the water. Now turn left under a little bridge with the **Hermitage** buildings on your right and the Hermitage Theatre on your left and sail up the Zimnaya Kanavka, the Winter Canal, until it meets up with the Moika River where you take a right and go under the **Pevchesky (Choristers') Bridge**. After the bridge on the left is the Capella, once the home of the Court Choir, now a concert hall. You should now be heading back towards the bridge and your point of disembarkation.

Birch branches for sale

It is an old Russian tradition to take a **steam bath** and the one I recommend is situated in Fon-arniy Pereulok, a 10-minute walk from the Narodny Most where you leave the boat. Keep walking up the Moika, in the same direction as the boat took you, past St Isaac's Square on your right. Take the next left after the square into Fonarniy Pereulok and the Baths are at No 1, on your right. Most hotels have their own steam rooms, saunas etc, but if you want to experience the real thing you should come here.

You should be sure to come equipped with your own soap, something to cover your head – a bath hat if you have one, but Russian women often wear woollen hats – your own soap and flip-flops if you have them; you are given a towel on arrival which looks more like a white sheet. Most important of all – but they won't turn you away if you don't have them – is a bundle of birch or oak branches. Often individual vendors will offer these for sale outside the door to the baths.

Don't expect luxury, although you must ask for 'luxe' when you go in. Walk up the main staircase, take a left at the top, walk along a short corridor and turn right at the end. This is where you should find the attendant with whom you leave your bags and hire a towel, etc. The door to the changing room is to the right. Pay at the end of your visit. Inside is a steam room, a sauna and a freezing cold small swimming pool, together with showers. It all looks pretty basic and old but it is worth the experience. I guarantee that you will feel really clean afterwards. The baths are open from 8am–10pm and closed on Monday. Sunday and Friday are women's days; the rest of the week is for men only.

Bliss in the baths: vodka, salad and hot wet air

9. Petrodvoretz – Peter's Palace

A boat or train trip to the most important of the palaces outside St Petersburg. Take food and drink.

–Start from the pier outside the Hermitage on Dvortsovaya Naberezhnaya or take a train from Baltic Station (Metro Station Baltiiskaya) to Novy Peterhof.–

If you are only in St Petersburg for a limited time, it can be difficult deciding which palace to visit – that is, if you are allowed to choose for yourself. Of all the palaces open to the public, **Petrodvoretz,** 29km (18 miles) west of the city on the Gulf of Finland, is considered to be the most important. The main palace is open 10am–5pm, closed on Monday and the last Tuesday of the month. One of the advantages of going under your own steam is that you can leave your choice until the last minute. A great deal depends on the weather and the time of year. It is fun to take the hydrofoil boat there in the summer months, but a ride on the electric railway can also be an adventure, and you will certainly feel less of a tourist.

The most striking feature of Petrodvoretz is its fountains but in the winter these are turned off. At the time of writing, restoration work is being carried out at the front of the palace, which affects the working of the splendid Grand Cascade Fountain. In Russia it is impossible to say when repair work will be completed but this should be within the next five years.

In the summer, you can take a boat to Petrodvoretz from the embankment in front of the Hermitage – there are two piers, serving two different excursions; the one you want is to the right, not the one

At Petrodvoretz

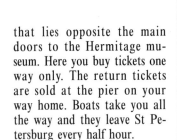

Grand Cascade fountains

that lies opposite the main doors to the Hermitage museum. Here you buy tickets one way only. The return tickets are sold at the pier on your way home. Boats take you all the way and they leave St Petersburg every half hour.

The palace at Petrodvoretz was built by Peter the Great in 1720 to the design of a French architect, Leblond, who unfortunately did not live to supervise its construction. The original palace was much simpler than the one you see today, which was enlarged and embellished by Elizabeth. But through the baroque glitz, traces of its founder and architect show through. All credit must go to them for choosing the magnificent site on a natural slope of ground – a Versailles by the sea – and for dreaming up and designing the intricate fountains, a major feat on land consisting of marshy clay.

If you look at old pictures of Petrodvoretz after World War II, you wonder how they ever rebuilt it. The scene after the German occupation was one of utter devastation. Some, but by no means all, of the treasures were smuggled out in time.

If you have come by boat and are walking up from the shore, you will see the **Grand Cascade** fountains – the focal point of the water gardens – as you approach the palace, with the famous **statue of Samson** rending apart the jaws of a lion.

The ticket offices, КАССА, are round the back of the palace.

Tourists are given priority over locals here (although they have to pay more) when it comes to being allowed in, so make yourselves heard. You pay more still if you go as part of an organised Intourist group.

Put on your *tapochki* (slippers) and set off, either listening to a tour in your own language if you are crafty, or on your own. If you want to study the palace in detail, there will be books and leaflets on sale. Don't miss the **oak staircase** and **oak study** which reflect Peter the Great's taste – some of the darker oak panels are the originals; also see the **Portrait Gallery** of 368 women in different costumes which Catherine brought in, and the **Throne Room** where Peter's original throne sits.

Don't leave without seeing the three pavilions in the gardens (all three are closed in winter). The first, the **Hermitage,** was where Peter entertained and a dumb waiter device operated as a section of the round table was lowered to be cleared and replenished below. The **Marly** is built in a simple, Dutch style and **Monplaisir**, by the water's edge, came to be Peter's favourite retreat – he could watch the sea from his bed. Marly is closed on Tuesday and the last Wednesday of the month, Monplaisir and the Hermitage are closed on Wednesday and the last Thursday of the month. If you take a walk behind the palace to the upper garden you will come across the newly created **Peterhof Palace Pharmacy** where you can try herbal drinks to cure all ailments.

10. Oranienbaum (formerly Lomonosov)

A summer trip to an unmodernised royal palace which is closed in winter. Take a picnic.

–Take a train from the Baltic Station to Oranienbaum station.–

This is a palace that is hardly visited by tourists. It is 12km (7½ miles) further down the coast from Petrodvoretz, so at a stretch,

Oranienbaum's Chinese Palace

The billiards room

the two visits could be combined. The station is on the same line as Petrodvoretz.

The palace was built by Alexander Menshikov and it was partly rivalry that goaded Peter into building Petrodvoretz. Catherine the Great spent much time here, as did her husband Peter III before she ousted him.

From **Oranienbaum I Station**, walk towards the recently re-opened **cathedral**. Next to the entrance is the grave of the Russian émigré Prince George Galitzine who spent most of his life in Britain. His mother was born and brought up in the Great Palace, and the last 30 years of his life were dedicated to encouraging Westerners to appreciate Russian culture.

Now cross the road and the entrance to the **park** is to your right. The park is open 9am–10pm, the palace and museums are open 11am–6pm, 11am–5pm on Monday, closed Tuesday and the last Monday of the month.

What is special about **Oranienbaum** is the fact that it escaped German occupation. Even though its main palace is closed and about to undergo restoration, it is interesting and curiously atmospheric to see an unmodernised and derelict building – and a splendid one at that.

Paddling in the park

But it has much more to offer – such as the fantastic **Chinese Palace** which, although restored, is the original. (Its Chinese décor is far more evident on the inside than from the outside.) Catherine had built an amazing, fairground-style roller coasting pavilion here with wooden toboggans. Sadly, this no longer stands, as it was later considered dangerous, although you can see a model of it in the blue and white pavilion, which is still intact. You can also hire a pedalo or rowing boat for a trip on the lake.

There are no restaurants here but if you haven't brought a picnic and are starving or in need of a hot drink, ask for the Pirozhko-vaya, the pie house, on your way back to the station, where you can buy cabbage pies and drink very sweet tea and coffee standing at a table. Delicious if you are hungry, if rather basic.

11. Repino, Estate of Ilya Ilych Repin

Combine a visit to an artist's home with a swim and a beach picnic. Take your own food and drink and a bathing costume on a hot day. Repino is 50km (31 miles) from the centre.

—From the Finland Station (metro station Ploshchad Lenina), take an electric train to Repino.—

A tour to Repin's house at Repino takes you north of the city to the Finnish Gulf or Karelian Isthmus. This excursion contrasts well with a visit to a palace – there is less grandeur for the eye to absorb, and with its wooden walls and simple design, you feel you are visiting the residence of a Russian, rather than a European. In the summer, there is a sandy beach nearby where you can picnic, as well as in the shady wooded grounds surrounding the house.

'Haven't you heard of Repin?' Russians ask, horrified. He was one of Russia's most famous and well-loved artists, although he is relatively unknown elsewhere. He lived from 1844 to 1930 and was one of the most prominent members of a group of artists called the *Peredvizhniki* or Wanderers. In the second half of the 19th century they rejected the restrictive and foreign-inspired classicism of the Academy of Arts in St Petersburg to create a new, realist and nationalist art that would serve the common man. They produced re-

Repin's House

alistic portrayals of inspiring or pathetic subjects, mainly from Russian middle-class and peasant life, in a literal, easily understood style. The movement dominated Russian art for 30 years and was the model for the Socialist realism of the Soviet Union.

Many of Repin's most famous pictures hang in the Russian Museum, such as *The Volga Boatmen*, *The Zaporozhian Cossacks write a Letter to the Turkish Sultan*, and *Portrait of Vladimir Stasov*.

If you have time before you take your train from the **Finland Station**, look at the huge bust of Lenin (unveiled in 1926) in front of the station, one of the few left in the city. It was here that Lenin arrived from Switzerland on 3 April 1917 and delivered his first revolutionary speech in Russia from an Austin armoured car.

Take the train to **Repino Station** (about three quarters of an hour). When you get to the station, cross the road in front of you and walk straight through some woods in the direction of the coast until you come to a main road. You can walk from here (turn left and carry straight on until you come to some wooden gates on the left hand side) or take three stops on the bus to just outside the gates. Remember to ask for *Penaty* or *Dom Repina* – **Repin's**

Repin's studio with his last self-portrait

house. It is open from 10am–6pm, closed on Tuesday. The park opens from 10am–8pm.

Go through the wooden gates and follow the path through the woods until you see a wooden house inside which you will find the КАССА and your *tapochki* – slippers. Ask for a cassette guide in your own language – the museum is proud of all the different languages they have available.

Repin spent the last 30 years of his life painting, entertaining and writing his memoirs. His guests included Maxim Gorky, the scientist Ivan Pavlov, the actor Fiodor Shaliapin and the poets Sergei Yesenin and Vladimir Mayakovsky. He set his own rules for entertaining whereby guests had to look after themselves, hence the messages over the brass gong as they entered: 'Self help... Take off your coats and galoshes yourself... Give a smart beat on the gong...' If anyone broke the rules of the special round table in the dining room, he had to get up on to the rostrum which stood in the corner and make a speech.

At the end of your tour, make sure you see the film of Repin and his friends, taken towards the end of his life.

Repin is buried in his garden – or estate. Despite his almost Tolstoyan wish for self-help and simplicity, he has given parts of his estate some very pretentious names – 'Homer's Sward', 'Scheherazade's Tower' etc – but its layout is neither pretentious nor grandiose.

As you come out of the gates at the end of your visit, cross the road and keep walking through the trees. You will soon find yourself – rather unexpectedly – standing on a sandy beach. If you get lost simply ask for the *Plyazh* – beach. Russians complain that the sea here is polluted, and it is best always to swim in the lakes, but despite this, the beaches along this coast are still popular resorts and **Solnechnoye**, in particular, on the same train line, can always be recommended.

Shopping

St Petersburg is hardly a city you visit for a shopping experience, but there are all sorts of interesting things that you can buy here nevertheless. There is still a big difference between what can be bought for the rouble and what can be bought for the dollar. If it is souvenirs you want, you will have no trouble – it's not all Gorby dolls. As a tourist, you are encouraged to spend money wherever you go.

Communist memorabilia

In the past, souvenirs were sold in special tourist shops called *Beriozkas*, which means little birch tree, or in orderly kiosks outside museums. Now, with the market economy, there are stalls everywhere, particularly outside tourist spots. Before you even get into the Peter and Paul Fortress, or wander peacefully around the Alexander Nevsky Monastery, you will urgently be encouraged to spend, spend, spend.

Not that *Beriozkas* are obsolete. They can be found in every hotel, and stock more goods than ever before, especially souvenirs. And you don't have to worry about bringing the right things to Russia anymore – *Beriozkas* also stock most essentials, from toothpaste to travelling irons and foodstuffs such as coffee, tea, fruit juice, cereal, even sugar and basic chemist items. Like any duty free shop, they sell alcohol, cigarettes and scent. You will have to go to the Russian shops to buy

Typical Russian doll

dairy products and bread and there are now western-style supermarkets as well.

What is there to buy here? Folk art seems to predominate in the form of *palekh* and woodwork. *Palekh* used to be a school of icon painting and is now the word used to describe intricate painting of enamelled wooden boxes. But most widespread, and cheaper, are the painted bowls, wooden spoons and boxes – even rings for your fingers – from Khokhloma.

You can also find attractive china, over-the-top teapots and embroidered linens. When it comes to clothing, you can choose between furs, T-shirts and army uniforms – soldier's hats, belts and coats. There are many lavish coffee-table books, printed in various languages. If it's trinkets you are looking to buy, there are endless badges, cigarette lighters and key rings. And you won't have to look very far for a samovar or a balalaika (a string instrument). The image of Lenin is still around, particularly on badges and on old flags – but selling out fast.

If you are an imaginative and adventurous shopper, then you should check out the Russian shops. The system there is to pay first at the till, then take your ticket to the cashier who will wrap up what you have bought. It's much cheaper to buy postcards in this way than in hotels. Rouble shops often sell the same souvenirs as in the *Beriozkas*, for much lower prices. I have listed the main stores, but if you feel like browsing, the main shopping streets are the Nevsky and Liteiny Prospekts, and Bolshoi Prospekt on the Petrograd side.

Caviar gives you strength

The Russian customs regulations are unpredictable here, ranging from extremely strict to incredibly lax. People who have visited Russia in the past will tell you how they managed to take a variety of items out of the country with no trouble whatsoever. Others will complain of how a beautiful old samo-

Typical souvenir stall

var or balalaika they bought was immediately confiscated. What you have to be careful of exporting is, first, anything antique – especially icons and valuable paintings; second, fur; and third, caviar. (The machine that photographs your luggage as you leave the country is quick to pick up the fish logo on the tins.)

However, if you can prove that you have paid in hard currency by showing your receipt, you should have no trouble and may well be able to take out a limited amount of, say, caviar. Please check with your tour operator on what is permitted at the time of your visit. As prices and laws are changing rapidly, any precise information given here may soon become out of date.

Beriozkas

Beriozkas are situated in every hotel. You don't have to be staying at the hotel to shop there. The Hotels Moskva, Astoria, Grand Hotel Europe and Pribaltiskaya stock foodstuffs as well as souvenirs. Many museums sell books, calendars, posters and postcards.

Souvenir stalls

The best market for souvenirs is in **Klenovaya Alleya** (Maple Alley). This small alley is often not marked on maps. To get there, walk from the Engineers' Castle with the statue of Peter I behind you, in the direction of the Manege flanked on each

Matrushka dolls

side by trees. The alley stall-holders have a wide selection of goods. Bargain hard; they'll want dollars. Original paintings are sold along the Nevsky Prospekt. Paintings and posters can be bought in literary museums, such as the Dostoevsky House and Anna Akhmatova House. Western shops such as Lancôme and Agfa are on the Nevsky Prospekt.

GOSTINNY DVOR
35 Nevsky Prospekt
Very large department store. Try out the kitchen or toy department. Also has good paper products, drawing books.

PASSAGE
48 Nevsky Prospekt
Much like Gostinny Dvor; specialises in women's clothes.

ISSKUSTV
16 Nevsky Prospekt
Art books, posters, postcards.

DOM KNIGI
28 Nevsky Prospekt
A selection of posters, postcards and maps.

ANTIKVARNAYA KNIGA
18 Nevsky Prospekt
Secondhand books.

BUKINIST
59 Liteiny Prospekt
Secondhand books.

MELODY
32/34 Nevsky Prospekt
Records.

RAPSODY
l3 Ulitsa Bolshaya Konnushennaya (Zhelyabova)
Sheet music, records and antiques.

10-10 GALLERY
10 Pushkinskaya (room 10)
Art Gallery. Closed at weekends.

FLOWERS HALL
2 Ulitsa Potemkinskaya

YAHONT (AMBER)
24 Bolshaya Movskaya Ulitsa
Jewellery shop inside former Fabergé building.

Shopping for food
Main fruit and vegetable markets:

VASILEOSTROVSKY
18 Bolshoi Prospekt (Vasilievsky Island)

KUZNECHNY
3 Kuznechny Pereulok

SYTNY
Sytninskaya Square (Petrograd Island)

The Passage department store

Russian bread, is extremely good and bread shops, *Bulochnaya*, can be found all over town. If you are unable to speak any Russian, write down the price for the cashier. Then exchange the receipt for bread.

Supermarkets
Foreign imported produce

BABYLON SUPERMARKET
69 Nevsky Prospekt and *54/56 Maly Prospekt (Petrograd side)*
Open 10am-9pm

COSMOS
76 Nevsky Prospekt
24 hour

STOCKMANN
1 Finlandskiy Prospekt (Vyborg side) ·
10am-9pm

The restaurant scene is improving fast but the city is still divided between the European and the Russian worlds, although European restaurants have by law to accept the rouble equivalent of a European priced bill. As a foreigner, it is much easier to eat in a western-style restaurant: the menu will be translated, the staff will speak your language and you won't be turned away at the door and told the place is full up or have to resort to bribery. You can sometimes pay by credit card but check in advance, and, providing there is no floor show drowning out conversation, these venues are suitable for business meetings. However, you won't always get a traditional Russian meal. All hotels have their own restaurants.

Russian restaurants can be divided into two categories: the traditional Russian restaurant, and the cooperative, private café. Sometimes the two styles merge, with pleasant results.

Fast food has arrived

Traditional Russian can mean a full night out with dancing and you should book in advance, through a hotel service bureau if you prefer. Meals are divided into many courses. *Zakuski* – starters – consist of an assortment of small dishes, from cold meat and fish, to hard-boiled eggs with red and black caviar. Sometimes restaurants overdo these and you will find far too much food laid out on your table when you arrive. To avoid this, ask for a *chisti stol* – a clear table – when you book. Then there is a soup course – *Schi* (cabbage soup) or *Bortsch*; salads; a meat dish – often *Kotleti* or cutlets – and a sweet pud-

Window at Demyanova Ukha

ding, often ice-cream. *Gribi so Smetani* – mushrooms with sour cream – is an old favourite, as are *Pelmeni* – ravioli.

The choice of alcoholic drink can be limited to champagne or sweet wines. *Kvas* – the national drink – has a beer-like, yeasty taste and soft drinks made with berries are often served, some much better than others. Many restaurants now stock carbonated drinks like Pepsi and Fanta.

The cooperative private cafés serve the best food. You have to order and pay at the counter, then the food is be brought to your table. No need to book in advance. If you persevere this can be very rewarding – and cheaper. It is difficult to predict how permanent such cafés will be, but some are included that seem secure. They are best at lunch time, and do not usually stay open late at night.

There are many functional eating places in the city, including *Stolovayas* – dining rooms which operate a cafeteria system; *Pirozhkovayas* – pie houses where you eat your cabbage pie and drink sweet tea or coffee standing at a circular table; *Molochnayas* (*Moloko* means milk), where dairy products such as semolina are served; and *Blinnayas* – pancake houses. Most of these places are quite basic, but when you're hungry and cold, a *pirog* – pie – can go down quite well.

Beware of ice, which is made with city water. Tip as you would in Europe. Most places close between lunch and dinner, and washroom facilities leave much to be desired.

Western Restaurants
Expensive

GRAND HOTEL EUROPE
1-7 Ulitsa Brodskovo (Mikhailovskovo)
Tel: 312-0072
Still aspires to be grand, as in the good old days. Attractive art nouveau decor. European-style food. Good breakfasts.

IMPERIAL RESTAURANT
1st floor, Nevsky Palace Hotel
57 Nevsky Prospekt
Tel: 311-6366
European menu. Open 7am-11pm.

DADDY'S
73 Moskovsky Prospekt
Tel: 298-9552
American-style steak house.

PICCOLO RESTAURANT
Olympia Hotel
Ploshchad Morskoy Slavy
Tel: 119-6800
Russian, European. Good breakfast.

Moderate

CHAIKA
14 Canal Griboedova (Ekaterinski Canal)
Tel: 312-4631
Pub interior. German beer.11am-3am.

NEVSKY 40
40 Nevsky Prospekt
Tel: 312-2457
Menu includes Russian, Italian and Asian dishes

SCHWABSKY DOMIK
28/19 Novocherkassy Prospekt
Tel: 528 2211
Russian-German cuisine. Open from noon-midnight.

Pancakes (bliny) and caviar

PIZZA EXPRESS
23 Podolskaya Ulitsa
Tel: 316-0217
If you feel like staying in you can also dial-a-pizza.

CHOPSTICKS (GRAND HOTEL EUROPE)
1-7 Mikhailovskaya Ulitsa
Tel: 119-6000
Recommended Chinese. Open 1pm-11pm.

JOHN BULL PUB
79 Nievsky Prospekt
Tel: 164-9877
English-style pub serving bar food. Also has restaurant. Open midday-midnight.

TANDOOR
2 Vosnesensky Prospekt
Tel: 312 3886
Indian Tandoori. Open from midday-11pm.

Russian restaurants
Expensive

RESTAURANT ST PETERSBURG
5 Griboedov/Ekaterinski Canal
Tel: 314 4947
Grand decor. Live music. Candlelight. Open noon-2am.

Moderate

IMPERIAL
53 Kamenoostrovsky Prospekt (Ulitsa Professora Popova). Petrograd side.
Tel: 234-1742
Small establishment. Decorated in style of the tsars. Classical music.

DOM ARCHITECTURI – HOUSE OF ARCHITECTS
52 Bolshay Morskaya
For architects, but public admitted. Beautiful interior, average food. Peaceful. Closed Sundays.

TETE A TETE
65 Boslhoi Prospekt (Petrograd side)
Tel: 232-7548
A must. Romantic, dimly-lit. Each table designed for two people only – but can ask for more. Good food. Open 1pm–1am.

STARAYA DEREVNYA
72 Ulitsa Savushkina (Petrograd side)
Tel: 239 9000.

DEMYANOVA UKHA
(Demyan's fish soup)
53 Kronversky Prospekt (Petrograd side)
Tel: 232 8090
Small, well-run restaurant serving excellent fresh fish from Lake Ladoga.

CAFE LITERATURNOYE
18 Nevsky Prospekt
Tel: 312-6057/7137
Attractive interior, chamber orchestra. Cover charge.

Café cadets

VICTORY RESTAURANT
24 Kamenoostrovsky Prospekt (Petrograd side)
Tel: 232-4143
Russian, German cuisine.

RESTORAN NA FONTANKA
77 River Fontanka
Tel: 310-2547
Dark interior swathed with material. Piano by day, live music at night. Open 10am–11pm.

European cafés

SADKOS (GRAND HOTEL EUROPE)
1-7 Mikhailovskovo Ulitsa/Ulitsa Brodskovo
Tel: 119-6000
Café/bar food. Open noon–12.30am.

BASKIN ROBBINS
79 Nevsky Prospekt
Ice cream. Open 10am-10pm.

BRASSERIE (GRAND HOTEL EUROPE)
1–7 Mikhailovskovo Ulitsa/Ulitsa Brodskovo
Tel: 119-6000
Russian and European food. Open midday-11pm.

Russian cafés

CAFÉ CAMEYA
32 Ulitsa Furmanova
Serves imaginative food. Open noon–11pm.

CAFÉ DRUZHBA
75 Nevsky Prospekt
Nothing fancy. Open noon–12am

CAFÉ IVERIA
35 Ulitsa Marata
This café specialises in Georgian cuisine. Open 11am–9.30pm.

CAFÉ 'PARAKAR'
Furshtadtskaya Ulitsa/Petra Lavrovo
Pleasant open-air summer café. Open all night.

14 RIVER FONTANKA
Nameless small café which is well run. You will find the entrance under the arch. Lots of fresh vegetables. Open 2pm–11pm.

Tea and Cakes

CAFÉ 01
5 Ulitsa Karavannaya/Tolmachoya
Reliably good food. Open noon–11pm.

CAFÉ KRUNK
Solianoe Pereulok
Reportedly good. Open Midday–9pm.

CAFÉ OT RESTORAN ST PETERSBURG
4 Griboedov/Ekaterinski Canal
Open 4pm–9pm.

PIROZHKOVAYA
47 Liteiny Prospekt
Basic.

Roubles will do

Nightlife in Russia can take on many forms and descriptions and, after the restrictions of the past, there are many new possibilities. If you visit the city in June, during the White Nights Festival, when it never gets dark, the city hardly sleeps. In the winter the fun goes on, but it's harder to leave your warm room. One of the key things to remember is that you are on many islands, and you can get marooned – the bridges go up to let the ships through in the middle of the night. Before going anywhere very late at night, check bridge times (they vary between approximately 2–5am).

However, most of the organised nightlife ends before you get cut off. If you have tickets to the ballet, opera or a classical music con-

The end of a fine performance

cert the performance usually starts around 7pm and is over by 9.30pm, giving you plenty of time to move on to the next thing. Restaurants close around midnight, although the ones with built-in discotheques and floor shows will stay open much longer (see restaurant section). Please check times before you go as they can be variable.

Many hotels arrange their own nightlife in bars and discotheques. The late night bars are reportedly good in the St Petersburg, Moskva, Pribaltiskaya and Pulkovskaya hotels. If you go out for a meal in a Russian restaurant this can well turn into a whole evening's event with music and dancing.

The club scene is thriving at the moment – young people are hungry for it. Although the increasing accessibility of Western music and culture makes you wonder if you are in Russia or Europe or the States, there are some interesting new and entirely original Russian bands which have emerged from the underground scene. Unfortunately, many clubs do not advertise themselves and venues continually change. Much is still done by word of mouth, and will not be advertised. Big raves are becoming increasingly popular, and the town has incredible venues to accommodate large crowds. There are more organised venues for those who like jazz and rock.

Remember to be careful on the street. St Petersburg used to be one of the safest cities. The metro is still regarded as the safest means of transport late at night and taxis are to be avoided if you are on your own. The metro closes at 1am and reopens at 6am. Buses also run until 1am. Taxis keep going all night.

The city often looks beautiful at night – under the snow, or during the White Nights. During this time, boat trips can be arranged late at night. Check for details through a hotel service bureau for the larger boats, or ask one of the taxi-boat drivers. If you don't feel like clubbing or sitting in a theatre, why not walk, and, making sure you are on the right island, watch the bridges lift and the boats go through.

The Ballet

Don't get confused – the Kirov is now called the Mariinsky Theatre. The ballet now enjoys such huge international fame that it is often on tour so you may well not be seeing the real thing. But the theatre in itself is spectacular with its beautiful auditorium, and if you do get seats, it is still considered a great privilege. As it is practically impossible to get seats for roubles you would do better

In the orchestra pit

to book through the tourist offices in any hotel – but make sure you do so well in advance. Tickets are extremely expensive, but cheaper ones can often be bought on the door – unofficially. The tickets look like old-fashioned bus tickets; check that the date is right.

THE MARIINSKY THEATRE (former Kirov)
1 Teatralnaya Ploshchad
The finest operas and ballets are performed here. Famous dancers such as Pavlova, Nijinsky made their débuts and former members include Nureyev and Makarova. Seats 1,800.

THE MALY (small) THEATRE OF OPERA AND BALLET
1 Ploshchad Iskusstvo
Second only to the Kirov. Seats 1,200.

HOUSE OF OFFICERS (DOM OFITSEROV)
20 Liteiny Prospekt
Also ballet.

Concert Halls

St Petersburg enjoys a rich musical tradition. Although there are ticket offices in town (Nevsky Prospekt 42) the best way to find out the details is to go to the Concert Halls in the daytime (after 11am) and ask what they are showing. Check the companies are not on tour.

OKTYABRSKY CONCERT HALL
6 Ligovsky Prospekt

Huge modern building (1967). Seats 4,000. Very good concerts both classical and modern. Also ballets.

THE MALY PHILARMONIA
30 Nevsky Prospekt
Small hall of the Philharmonia. The pianist Anton Rubinstein made his début here.

THE SMOLNY CATHEDRAL
3 Ploshchad Rastrelli
Concerts and choral recitals.

THE ACADEMIC CAPELLA (Glinka)
20 Naberezhnaya Reki Moiki
Glinka and Rimsky Korsakov taught here. Home of the former court choir. Classical and contemporary concerts.

SHOSTAKOVICH PHILARMONIA
*2 Mikhailovskaya Ulitsa/
Ulitsa Brodskovo*
Originally the Club of the Gentry. Famous for its connection with clas-

The Mariinsky Theatre

74

sical music staged then and now in the Bolshoi (large) hall. Wagner, amongst others, conducted here.

For Children

THE BOLSHOI PUPPET THEATRE
10 Ulitsa Nekrasova
Founded in 1931.

The Circus

CIRCUS
3 Naberezhnaya Reki Fontanki
Former home of the Cinizelli Circus.

Theatres

THE STATE ACADEMIC THEATRE OF COMEDY
56 Nevky Prospekt
Soviet and foreign drama.

ALEXANDRINSKY THEATRE (PUSHKIN DRAMA THEATRE)
2 Ploshchad Ostrovskovo
Ballet as well as theatre.

THE BOLSHOI DRAMATIC THEATRE
65 Naberezhnaya Reki Fontanki
Famous for its productions under the late G A Tovstonogov.

MALY DRAMATIC THEATRE
18 Ulitsa Rubinshteina

SHARMANKA
7 Moskovsky Prospekt
Russia's first cinematic theatre, now enjoying international success.

Clubs

THE TUNNEL
Corner of Lynbansky Perenlok and Zverinskaya Ulitsa. (Petrograd side)
Trance, House, Ambient. Located in underground bomb shelter. Thursday, 7pm–midnight. Friday and Saturday, midnight–6am

JAZZ CLUB
27 Zagorodny Prospekt
Live bands. Daily except Mondays. Open 2pm–8pm

ROCK CLUB
13 Ulitsa Rubinshteina
Good place to come to hear live Russian bands. Open 8pm–11pm.

TAMTAM CLUB
Corner of Maly Prospekt and 17th Linia
Vasilievsky Island
Live bands, dance flour. This popular club was founded by ex-member of a Russian underground group. Thursdays, Fridays and Saturdays 8pm–11pm.

Circus poster

GETTING THERE

When to Visit

The best times to visit St Petersburg are mid summer and mid winter. It is hard to be too specific about the weather in a city that is so exposed to the elements. Although there are distinct seasons, there are often freak weather conditions. A strong wind often blows in from the sea, which can be pleasant in the summer when it is hot, but less so in winter.

The long days of summer from the end of May to the end of July are a feature of a traditionally romantic time when the atmosphere is festive. The weather can be hot during the months of June, July and August, averaging between 11–21°C (52–70°F). September can also be golden and pleasant, averaging between 9–15°C (48–59°F).

The city is often less crowded in summer, when people go on holiday and visit their dachas outside the town. Remember that you are near the coast, which means sunbathing and beaches. Unfortunately the sea water is polluted, but there are many clear lakes.

Snow begins to fall in November and by December it settles and freezes, not thawing until March. With its pastel colour schemes, the city looks incredibly beautiful under the snow if you don't mind the

Commuter train

cold. December and January are the coldest months, when the temperature falls as low as -17°C (1°F). Avoid October to November, before the snow has really settled, and March (when it is thawing and slushy underfoot). Spring begins at the end of March.

Ticket to ride

Visas and Customs

You cannot enter the country without a visa. Apply at least two weeks before your visit, or a month in advance if you are travelling independently. White customs declarations forms will be issued on arrival. State how much currency you are bringing into the country and declare valuable items such as jewellery or computer equipment. If possible, show receipts that cover these items.

Don't lose the customs form as it will be needed when you leave the country to demonstrate that you are not leaving with more money than when you entered. You should also present it to the bank when you change money (see currency section for further details). It is unlikely that your bags will be searched at customs, but pack them in such a way that it won't be a disaster if they are.

When you leave the country, the same procedure applies in reverse. Fill out another form and present it with your first. Keep all receipts of goods you have bought during your visit (see shopping section).

Clothing

The most important thing is to be comfortable, so it is essential to have good walking shoes. In the winter it is important that you have shoes that are waterproof, warm and easy to walk in. There is nothing worse than having cold, wet feet in the snow. Other winter essentials are a very warm coat, a hat (preferably to cover your ears) and gloves. Buildings are centrally heated, and most have an efficient *Garderob* or cloakroom system, where you can safely leave your belongings. Carry a spare pair of indoor shoes in winter, as you may not want to trudge round a museum or watch the ballet in moon boots.

Even if you are travelling in mid-summer, bring a sweater and jacket. An umbrella can also be a lifesaver. Bring sunglasses, suncream, sunhat and a swimming costume.

Russians like to be smartly dressed, particularly in the evenings, but on the street, comfort is the highest priority. Formal dress is obligatory for business meetings.

Useful Items

In summer the mosquitoes can be a real pest, although they do not carry malaria. Take both insect gel and a mosquito coil for your room at night. If you are staying in a hotel the following can be invaluable: soft loo paper, a penknife, a bathplug, liquid detergent, a mini-boiler or small kettle, a knife and fork. For picnics it is useful to have a thermos. If you intend to shop at a market, take plastic bags. Always keep jars to carry sour cream, bottles to store boiled water. Packet soups, coffee, tea and hot drinks can be life-savers.

Photography

Bring your own film, though there is a limited choice in duty free shops. Agfa has now opened a shop on the Nevsky Prospekt.

Electricity

Bring a continental adaptor plug for a hairdryer, travelling iron or electric razor. The standard voltage is 220 volts.

Time Differences

St Petersburg is three hours ahead of British summertime and GMT, two hours ahead of other European cities, and eight hours ahead of New York. Therefore, when it is noon in St Petersburg it is

Outside Kazan Cathedral

9am in London, 10am in most European capitals and 4am in New York. Summertime, when clocks are put forward by one hour, runs 31 March–30 September.

USEFUL INFORMATION

Specialist Museums

ANNA AKHMATOVA MUSEUM
Sheremetev Palace, Naberezhnaya Fontanka entrance through courtyard at 51 Liteiny Prospekt
10.30am–6.30pm, closed Monday and last Wednesday of month.

BOTANICAL MUSEUM OF THE RUSSIAN ACADEMY OF SCIENCES
2 Ulitsa Professora Popova (Petrograd side).

LENIN MEMORIAL MUSEUM
Ploshchad Proletarskoy Dictatony
Entrance behind Lenin statue.

MUSEUM OF ARTILLERY, ENGINEERS AND SIGNALS
Kronverskaya Naherezhnaya (Petrograd side)
Behind Peter and Paul fortress.

YUSUPOV PALACE
96 Naberezhnaya Moiki
Where Rasputin was murdered. Highly recommended. (Foreign-speaking guides – tel: 311 5353. Arrange in advance.)

Other Attractions

ZOO
1 Alexandrinsky Gardens

PLANETARIUM
4 Alexandrinsky Gardens

RELIGION

Religion, declared 'the opium of the people' by Karl Marx, is now playing an increasingly important role in people's lives. Under Gorbachev many churches were reopened for worship. Most Russian Orthodox churches have a morning Divine Liturgy at 10am and an evening service at 6pm. Women should cover their heads in churches; mini-skirts and shorts tend to offend. If you wish to take photographs, ask first.

Russian Orthodox
CATHEDRAL OF THE TRINITY
Ploshchad Alexander Nevskovo

CATHEDRAL OF ST NICHOLAS
Ploshchad Kommunarov

CATHEDRAL OF THE TRANSFIGURATION
Ploshchad Radischeva

VLADIMIR CHURCH
Vladimirskaya Ploshchad

Catholic
7 Kovensky Pereulok

Baptist
29a Bolshaya Ozernaya Ulitsa

Mosque
7 Maxim Gorky Prospekt

Synagogue
2 Lermontovsky Prospekt

MONEY MATTERS

Currency

Hard currency is much in demand, but you will need roubles. All hotels have banks, many open throughout the day. There are many new banks in the city where foreign money can be exchanged such as Ulitsa Bolshaya Morskaya 29, 4 Mikhailovskaya Ulitsa and 7 Ploshchad Ostrovskovo

The advantage of changing money in a bank is that it will be officially recorded on your customs declaration form enabling you to change roubles back into hard currency when you leave. It is illegal to import or export roubles. You may bring in as much hard currency as you want as long as it is declared (see also visa section).

Safety

It is unwise to change money on the street. Beware of pickpockets. It is often safer to cross large roads where an underground passageway is available. Carry a card which says, in Russian, the address where you are staying.

Credit Cards

Western restaurants usually accept major bank cards and traveller's cheques but be sure to confirm when you book. Hard currency can be drawn from your account on a bank card – but this service is limited and can take up to 24 hours.

Tipping

There is a tipping system in Russia and as in most European countries it is about 10 percent. In hotels, it is best to tip in dollars or give a small present. In a rouble restaurant, leave roubles. If you have agreed a fare with a taxi driver there is no need to tip. A packet of cigarettes or a dollar or two can still get you into a 'fully booked' restaurant.

GETTING AROUND

Geography

St Petersburg, Russia's largest seaport and second largest city, lies on a parallel 60° north of the equator – the same latitude as Alaska and Oslo. Finland lies 160km (99 miles) to the north.

The city straddles 101 islands at the mouth of the great River Neva which sweeps majestically through its centre, emptying Lake Ladoga 74km (45 miles) to the east into the Gulf of Finland to the west. Granite embankments contain

Old and New Street Names of St Petersburg

Old Name	New Name
Maxim Gorky Prospekt	Kronversky Prospekt
Ulitsa Pestelya	Ulitsa Panteleymonskaya
Prospekt Mayorova	Voznesensky Prospekt
Ploschad Mira	Sennaya Ploschad
Ploschad Dekabristov	Senatskaya Ploschad
Ploschad Vosstania	Znamenskaya Ploschad
Ulitsa Rakova	Italianskaya Ulitsa
Ulitsa Dzherzhinskovo	Ulitsa Gorokhovaya
Canal Griboedova	Ekaterinsky Canal
Kirovsky Prospekt	Kamenoostrovsky Prospekt
Kirovsky Bridge	Troitsky Bridge
Ulitsa Petra Lavrova	Furshtadtskaya Ulitsa
Ulitsa Zhelyabova	Bolshaya Konyushennaya Ulitsa
Ulitsa Tolmacheva	Karavannaya Ulitsa
Ulitsa Soyuza Svyazi	Pochtantskaya Ulitsa
Ulitsa Brodskovo	Mikhailovskaya Ulitsa
Ulitsa Khalturina	Millionnaya Ulitsa
Karta Marska Prospekt	Bolshoy Sampsonievsky Prospekt
Ulitsa Gertzena	Bolshaya Morskaya Ulitsa
Ulitsa Gogolya	Malaya Morskaya Ulitsa

the 65 rivers, canals, channels and streams which separate all the islands but flooding occurs when gales come in from the Baltic.

There are 365 bridges joining the islands. These waterways, Lake Ladoga and the sea all freeze over in winter but icebreakers keep the port open throughout the year.

From the Admiralty on the south embankment, the main streets radiate as spokes of a wheel; the canals and other streets cross these spokes running parallel to the main channel of the Neva.

The streets are re-adopting their pre-revolutionary names, which can be confusing, particularly as many maps will not show the new names. The most important name changes appear in the chart on the previous page.

If in doubt, ask for the old names – they are fixed in people's minds. The following may also be useful:

Ulitsa – street
Ploshchad – square
Pereulok – small street
Naberezhnaya – embankment
Most – bridge
Ostrov – island
Prospekt – prospect
Linia – line

Taxis

Taxis are usually pale yellow with a 'T' sign and a chequered light or strip on the side. Taxi meters and ranks have long since gone out of use. Taxis that congregate outside hotels will always demand a higher price, so it is cheaper to stick your

Taxis are mainly for foreigners

arm out on the street. Always bargain. It will be easier if you learn a few Russian numbers so that you can agree a price before you get in. Or take a notepad and write the figure out. The driver may well ask you for dollars, but try to insist on roubles. As prices continue to rise it is impossible to give a realistic figure so you will have to ask for advice when you get there.

Metro

Runs from 5.30am-12.30am approximately. It is fast, cheap, clean and famous for its architecture and design. It is well worth mastering, although it can seem daunting at first if you don't understand the cyrillic alphabet. If in doubt, avoid journeys where you have to change to another line. Metro stations are marked on the road with an 'M' sign. You buy your *talon* or token at the kiosk, then feed it into the barrier; a green light comes on and you walk through onto a fast-moving escalator. Keep to the right hand side on the escalator.

The Electric Railway

Many locals use this service to take them to their dachas. Local trains run from the Finland, Vitebsk, and Baltic Stations, all of which are served by their own metros. It is the cheapest way to travel out to one of the palaces. The ticket system operates here so make sure you buy a return.

Buses, Trams and Trolleybuses

Run from 6–1am. If you decide to make full use of this system during your stay, try to acquire a special map called 'Marshruti Gorodskovo Transporta – Trolleibus, Avtobus i Trambai' – Town transport routes for Trolleybuses, Buses and Trams. Without such a map, you could get lost. Sometimes they are easy to buy, sometimes they fall out of circulation. Ask at a hotel service bureau.

During the rush hour the buses and

Splendid surroundings at the Pushkin metro station

trolleybuses are very crowded, trams less so. Look for an 'A' sign for a bus stop and a 'T' for a Trolleybus. The tram signs hang in the middle of the road on wires, also a 'T'. Tickets can be bought in strips from the conductor and to validate them you punch a hole in your ticket yourself on stapler-like machines hanging on the wall.

Car Hire

Enquire at a hotel service bureau. You will need an international driving licence and to have held your own licence for at least three years.

Boats

Regular boat trips with a Russian guide on large covered boats leave regularly from Dvortsovaya Naberezhnaya, in front of the Hermitage, and take you along four of the river embankments. Each trip lasts approximately one hour. There is also a covered boat excursion of the same duration which explores the rivers and canals from the Anichkov Bridge on the Nevsky Prospekt. Taxi-boats – smaller, open topped boats which seat up to ten people, can usually be found on Narodny Bridge as the Nevsky crosses the Moika Canal. Hydrofoil boats to Petrodvoretz also leave from outside the Hermitage,

from a different pier. Boats do not operate in winter or when it is windy. Taxi-boats demand hard currency, the others can be paid in roubles.

Bridges

The bridges open up in the early hours of the morning, some of them twice, to let ships through. Usual times range between 1.55–4.50am. Don't get stranded on the wrong island.

HOURS AND HOLIDAYS

Business Hours

Don't expect wonders when it comes to business hours – or for places to be open when they say they will. The sign *Na Remont* – under restoration – is an all too familiar one. Everywhere has its own

A *tour boat*

opening and closing times, so it is best to check times individually. In general, most department stores are open between 10am–9pm. Food shops open an hour or so earlier and close before 8pm, with a break between 2–3pm.

Make sure you get to museums at least half an hour before their official closing times or you will be refused admittance.

Check restaurant times individually on the day. Private cafés are not always predictable and generally close for an hour after they have served lunch and before they reopen for dinner.

Food markets are open between 8am–7pm. They close at 4pm on Sunday.

Public Holidays

Since the overthrow of communism it has become impossible to give specific dates although the festivals observed by the Russian Orthodox Church are taking on a new importance. The Orthodox Christmas falls on 7 January and Easter is a moveable feast. There is a New Year holiday on 1 January and International Women's Day is still celebrated on 8 March.

ACCOMMODATION

Although other travel organisations exist and new ones are forming all the time, Intourist is still the largest travel company in Russia with a huge network of offices and agents throughout the world. It organises group and individual travel and has its own hotels, most of which are graded using the star system. Unless you travel independently, Intourist appoints your hotel for you.

The two grandest, most luxurious and oldest hotels in the centre of St Petersburg are the Grand Hotel Europe, at Mikhailovskaya Ulitsa, and the Astoria, at Bolshaya Morskaya Ulitsa, both of which have recently been refurbished. The new Nevsky Palace, in Nevsky Prospekt, is of the same standard, together with the floating Olympia Hotel.

The Pribaltiskaya, an entirely modern hotel, is 7km (4½ miles) from the centre; the Pulkovskaya, 8km (5 miles) from the

centre, is near the airport. The Moskva and St Petersburg and Oktyabryskaya hotels may not always have bathplugs, but at least they have the advantage of being centrally placed. You will pay less to stay at the Karelia, but you will have to travel 10km (6 miles) to the centre and there is no metro nearby. With the exception of the Karelia, Intourist does not use the cheaper hotels listed, where standards will be pretty basic. (See listings below for details.)

Whilst Intourist does organise individual travel, it can be more expensive than group travel. Being part of a tour group does not restrict you from exploring the city on your own. Hotel prices can change literally overnight, so always check them thoroughly.

Hotels of all grades have a *Dezhurnaya,* or attendant, on each floor. They can provide you with boiled water, book phone calls and arrange for your laundry to be done.

ASTORIA
39 Bolshaya Morskaya Ulitsa
Tel: 311-4206

GRAND HOTEL EUROPE
1/7 Mikhailovskaya Ulitsa/
Ulitsa Brodskovo Tel: 119 6000

NEVSKY PALACE HOTEL
57 Nevsky Prospekt
Tel: 275 2001

HOTEL OLYMPIA (Floating)
1 Ploshchad Morskoy Slavy
Tel: 217 4416

Outside the Astoria

The Grand Hotel Europe

PRIBALTISKAYA
14 Ulitsa Korablestroiteley
Tel: 356 0263

PULKOVSKAYA
1 Ploshchad Pobedy
Tel: 264 5109

ST PETERSBURG
(former Leningrad)
5-2 Vyborgskaya Naberezhnaya
Tel: 542 9411

MOSKVA
2 Ploshchad Alexandra Nevskovo
Tel: 274 2115

SOVIETSKAYA
43 Prospekt Lermontovo
Tel: 114 0160

KARELIA
27/2 Ulitsa Tukhachevskaya
Tel: 226 5701

HOTEL DRUZHBA
4 Ulitsa Chapygina
Tel: 234 1844

DVORETZ MOLODYOZHY
47 Ulitsa Professor Popov
Tel: 234 3278

OCTYABRSKAYA
Ligovsky Prospekt
Tel: 277 6330

YANTN HOSTELS
3rd Sovyetskaya Ulitsa
Tel: 277 0569

HOLIDAY
Ulitsa Mikhailova 1
Tel: 572 7364

HEALTH AND EMERGENCIES

At present vaccinations and health certificates are not required. It is a good idea to take your own medicines although there are chemists selling foreign medicines for hard currency and you can find most things you need.

The most common ailment is mild stomach upset, but there is a more serious illness that can be picked up from drinking contaminated water containing the parasite *Giardia lamblia*. Avoid drinking unboiled water at all costs. Ideally, water should boil for 10 minutes. Purification tablets are no use and unboiled water is often used even in the best hotels to make ice. Beware of salads that look watery. But don't be too alarmed by the 'Leningrad water disease'. It won't kill you, although it can make life unpleasant.

Avoid drinking alcohol bought from street kiosks. And remember to ask your doctor what you should take with you as the recommended treatment.

The following are polyclinics which also stock foreign medicines. You will have to pay for medicines and in-patient treatment.

THE AMERICAN MEDICAL CENTRE
77 River Fontanka
Tel: 119 6101

Portrait artist on Nevsky Prospekt

N2

22 Moskovsky Prospekt
Tel: 292 6272
(24-hour emergency number: 292 6272/110 1102), ambulance and baby food.

STOLOMATOLOGICAL

13 10th Sovetskaya Ulitsa
Tel: 274 6480

Dentist

DINA INTERNATIONAL

186 Moskovsky Prospekt
Tel: 294 1249/294 1652

NORDMED

Tverskaya Ulitsa 12/15
Tel: 110 0206/110 0654
(Weekends and evenings)

DENTAL POLYCLINIC NO 3

Vasilievsky Ostrov 21-ya Linia, 12
Tel: 213 7551/213 5550
(Weekends and evenings)

DENTAL AND CONTACT LENS

Tel: 355 8388/218 4190

Eyes

VISOR

30 Liteiny Prospekt
Tel: 272 7642
10am–6pm; 10am–4pm, closed Saturday and Sunday

VISION EXPRESS

Lomonosova Ulitsa 5
Tel: 310 1595

English language news

Emergency Numbers (free of charge)

Fire 01
Police 02
Ambulance 03

Crime

St Petersburg used to be one of the safest cities in the world but is no longer. But it is not as dangerous as people say. In general, the laws of common sense apply. If something is stolen, report the theft to the police immediately and ensure that they issue you with a certificate showing the precise dates and times. Little may be done to retrieve your property but you can claim on your insurance. If you are travelling with a group such as Intourist, try to obtain a certificate from your tour operator or guide as well.

Public Toilets

Prepare yourself for the worst: the standard of many public toilets is utterly disgusting. There will not always be loo paper, so take your own. The cleanest loos are in the Grand Hotel Europe.

COMMUNICATIONS

You can choose between the expensive (hard currency) generally efficient system in a hotel or the cheaper (roubles) public post office, for all communications. Both have fax, telex and international phone and telegram facilities.

It is impossible to dial abroad direct from a public call box. Some hotels have their own telephone systems whereby they dial the number and you get through immediately. This can cost money. Ask, where possible, to be connected through Lenfincom. Less sophisticated hotels can book the call for you through an international operator. By far the cheapest way is to dial the operator yourself.

Post does eventually reach the outside world – but can take a couple of weeks. Use the blue post boxes.

If you want to make a local call there are many coin boxes. It's often easier to go into a hotel and ask to use their phone – local calls are then free of charge.

CENTRAL POST OFFICE
*9 Ulitsa Pochtantskaya
(Ulitsa Soyuza Svyazi)*
Open 9am–9pm; Sunday 10am–8pm

International Telephone Calls
To dial out of Russia dial 8 and then 10 followed by the country code. If you have difficulty call the operator on 315 0012.

Media
Some international newspapers are on sale in hotels. Also local papers will be on sale in different languages and often contain up-to-date information.

Radio and Television
If you bring a multi-band radio you can pick up many English-language broadcasts including BBC World Service (SW) and Voice of America (SW).

USEFUL ADDRESSES

Consulates

AUSTRIA
*Ulitsa Furshtadtskaya 43
Tel: 275 0496*

BULGARIA
*27 Ulitsa Ryleeva 27
Tel: 273 7347*

CANADA
*Grand Hotel Europe
Room 459
Tel: 312 0072 x 459*

CHINA
*12, 3rd Linia, Vasilievsky Island
Tel: 218 1721*

Forthcoming attractions

CUBA
*37 Ulitsa Ryleeva
Tel: 272 5303*

CZECH
*5 Tverskaya Ulitsa
Tel: 271 0459*

DENMARK
*Bolshaya Alleye 13
Tel: 234 3755*

ESTONIA
*Bolshaya Monetnaya Ulitsa 14
Tel: 233 5548*

FINLAND
*71 Ulitsa Chaikovskovo
Tel: 273 7321*

FRANCE
*15 Naberezhnaya Moika
Tel: 312 1130*

GERMANY
*39 Furshtadskaya
Tel: 273 5598*

GREAT BRITAIN
*Ploshchad Proletarskoi
Dictatury 5
Tel: 119 6036*

HUNGARY
*15 Ulitsa Marata
Tel: 312 6458*

INDIA
*Ulitsa Ryleeva 35
Tel: 272 1988*

ITALY
10 Teatralnaya Ploshchad
Tel: 312 2896

JAPAN
29 Naberezhnaya Moika
Tel: 314 1434

LATVIA
Galernaya Ulitsa 69
Tel: 315 1774

MONGOLIA
Tel: 153 8051

NETHERLANDS
Prospekt Morisa Toreza 118
Tel: 554 4900

POLAND
12/15th Ulitsa Sovetskaya
Tel: 274 4170

SOUTH AFRICA
Prospekt Morisa Toreza 118
Tel: 553 5718

SWEDEN
(V.O) 11, 10th Linia
Tel: 218 3526

US
15 Ulitsa Furshtadskaya
Tel: 274 8235/274 8689

MAPS

Maps can be bought in hotels and bookshops. Whilst they will list the main streets, the smaller ones may be omitted. Before you travel, try to get hold of the most detailed map of the city, the German 'Falkplan' map of St Petersburg, which is unlikely to be on sale in St Petersburg. As street names continue to change, it is often helpful to buy a pre-Revolutionary map so that you can compare the two.

LANGUAGE

It will help you enormously, particularly when using the metro and reading maps,

to have an understanding of the Cyrillic alphabet. Don't be daunted by it – once you have learnt it, you won't forget it.

SPORT

If you are a health fanatic and don't mind paying, try the health centres in the Grand Europe and Astoria Hotel or the swimming pools in town.

Swimming Pools
20 Bolshaya Raznochinnaya Street
44 Prospekt Dinamo (Krestovsky Ostrov)
38 Ulitsa Dekabristov
5a Novocherkassy Prospekt
3 Ulitsa Litovskaya

Spectator Sports
LENIN STADIUM
Petrovsky Ostrov, 2-g
(Also used for rock concerts)

KIROV STADIUM
Krestovsky Ostrov
Watch St Petersburg's soccer team, 'Zenith'.

JUBILEE SPORTS PALACE
18 Dobrolubov Street
Ice hockey

WINTER STADIUM
2 Manezhnaya Ploshchad

Horse Riding
As well as hiring tired, skinny-looking horses on the Nevsky Prospekt and in Palace Square, horses can be hired for hard currency 18km (11 miles) outside the city at the Olgino Motel and Campsite, Primorskoe Shosse, tel: 238 3132. (Electric train from the Finland Station to Olgino.) Ask at a hotel bureau for details. Also at Prostor-Park Riding School and Stables, 20 Krestovsky Ostrov, tel: 230 3988.

Skating and Skiing
For skating, there is a rink on Vasilievsky Island, 2, 15th line. Cross country skiing can be arranged from Olgino (see above). Again, ask a hotel service for details.

The main Russian organisations organising group travel are Intourist, CCTE, The Central Council for Tourism, and Sputnik. All have agents throughout the world. There are a growing number of tour operators specialising in individual travel and private accommodation. Try Lenart Tours, 40 Nevsky Prospekt (tel: 312 4837). Rail tickets can be bought direct at 24 Nabenezhnaya Kanal Griboedova. Go to the desk marked 'Intourist' upstairs.

FURTHER READING

Non-fiction

'Guide to a Renamed City' in *Less than One*, Joseph Brodsky. Penguin, 1986.

Imperial Splendour, George Galitzine. Viking, 1991.

One hot summer in St Petersburg, Duncan Fallowell, Cape 1994.

Pavlovsk: The Life of a Palace, Suzanne Massie. Hodder & Stoughton, 1990.

Peter the Great: His Life and Work, Robert K Massie. Abacus, 1981.

Russia, with Teheran, Port Arthur and Peking, Karl Baedeker, 1914. Reissued by David & Charles, 1971.

St Petersburg: A Travellers' Companion, Laurence Kelly. Constable, 1987

The Traveller's Yellow Pages and Handbook for St Petersburg, ed Michael R Dohan, 1993, Infoservices International, New York (tel: 516 549-0064).

Insight Guide: St Petersburg, Apa Publications, 1991.

The Orthodox Church, Timothy Ware, 1969.

The Russian Experiment in Art, Camilla Gray. Thames & Hudson, 1962.

Fiction

Among the Russians, Colin Thubron. Heinemann/Penguin, 1983.

Anna Karenina, Leo Tolstoy, 1876. Penguin.

Crime and Punishment, Fyodor Dostoevsky, 1866. Penguin.

Dead Souls, Nikolai Gogol, 1842. Penguin.

Eugene Onegin, Alexander Pushkin, 1831. Penguin.

Glas: New Russian Writing, ed Natasha Perova. UK subscriptions and enquiries (tel: 021 414 6044).

St Petersburg, Andrei Bely, 1916. Penguin.

Poetry

'The Bronze Horseman' (1859). Alexander Pushkin, Secker.

'The Twelve' (1918). Alexander Blok, Journeyman.

Going home

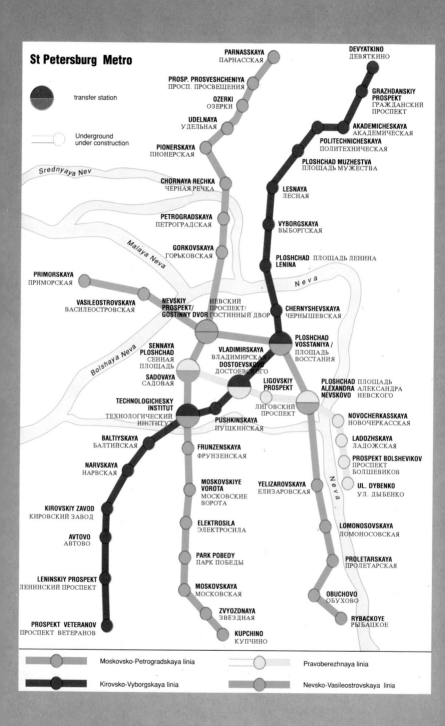

Art & Photo Credits

Photography	**Tony Perrottet** *and*
Page 59	**Fritz Dressler**
10, 12, 13T	**Grudenko**
14T&B	**Jürgens**
13B	**Wilhelm Klein**
Handwriting	**V Barl**
Production Editor	**Mohammed Dar**
Cover Design	**Klaus Geisler**
Cartography	**Berndtson & Berndtson**

INSIGHT GUIDES

COLORSET NUMBERS

You'll find the colorset number on the spine of each Insight Guide.

INSIGHT *Pocket* GUIDES

• •

United States: **Houghton Mifflin Company, Boston MA 02108**
Tel: (800) 2253362 Fax: (800) 4589501

Canada: **Thomas Allen & Son, 390 Steelcase Road East**
Markham, Ontario L3R 1G2
Tel: (416) 4759126 Fax: (416) 4756747

Great Britain: **GeoCenter UK, Hampshire RG22 4BJ**
Tel: (256) 817987 Fax: (256) 817988

Worldwide: **Höfer Communications Singapore 2262**
Tel: (65) 8612755 Fax: (65) 8616438

❝ I was first drawn to the Insight Guides by the excellent "Nepal" volume. I can think of no book which so effectively captures the essence of a country. Out of these pages leaped the Nepal I know – the captivating charm of a people and their culture. I've since discovered and enjoyed the entire Insight Guide Series. Each volume deals with a country or city in the same sensitive depth, which is nowhere more evident than in the superb photography. ❞

Sir Edmund Hillary